Loving Life

Loving Life

The Morality Of Self-Interest And The Facts That Support It

CRAIG BIDDLE

Glen Allen Press
Richmond, Virginia

Published by Glen Allen Press, P.O. Box 5274, Glen Allen, VA 23058.
Fourth printing 2009.

Publisher's Cataloging-in-Publication Data

    Biddle, Craig.
       Loving life : the morality of self-interest and the
    facts that support it / Craig Biddle.
       p. cm.
       Includes bibliographical references and index.
       LCCN 2001119589
       ISBN-10 0-9713737-0-1
       ISBN-13 978-0-9713737-0-9

       1. Egoism. 2. Ethics. I. Title.
    BJ1474.B53 2002   171'.9
              QBI01-201328

Attention educational organizations: Special discounts are available on bulk purchases of this book. For information, please contact Glen Allen Press, P.O. Box 5274, Glen Allen, VA 23058.

Acknowledgments

Many people, in various ways, have helped me in the process of writing this book, and I extend my gratitude to them all. There are, however, a few to whom I owe special thanks and acknowledgment.

First and foremost, I wish to thank my lovely wife, Sarah, who fueled and encouraged me throughout the project, reread the manuscript more times than I can remember, and made countless suggestions for improvement.

I want to acknowledge my enormous debt to Ayn Rand, on whose philosophy of Objectivism *Loving Life* is based. Her books taught me what in essence it means to love life and inspired me to write about it.

I am grateful also to Dr. Leonard Peikoff, whose books and lectures have helped me to better understand Ayn Rand's philosophy and the history of philosophy in general.

Finally, I want to thank my friend Robert Tracinski for his excellent editorial comments and for teaching me a great deal about writing.

The purpose of morality is to teach you, not to suffer and die, but to enjoy yourself and live.

—Ayn Rand

Contents

Introduction

Who Should Read This Book— And Why

If you want to live your life to the fullest, if you want to achieve the greatest happiness possible, this book is for you. It is about the essential means to that end: a proper code of values—a proper morality.

Contrary to popular myth, morality does not come from God; it is not a matter of divine revelation. Nor is it a matter of social convention or personal opinion. Being moral does not consist in obeying commandments, or in doing whatever is culturally accepted, or in doing whatever one wants to do. The rabbis, the priests, the relativists, and the subjectivists are wrong. Morality is not a matter of faith or conformity or feelings.

True morality is a matter of the factual requirements of human life and happiness. It is a matter of reason, logic, and the law of cause and effect. As such, it is an indispensable guide to living well and loving life. This is demonstrated in the pages ahead.

1

Religion Versus Subjectivism

Why Neither Will Do

"If there is no God, anything goes." This popular claim is an eloquent distillation of a deep-rooted false alternative wreaking havoc on human life and happiness. The adage compresses into a few words the age-old debate over whether morality is a matter of "divine commandments" or "human sentiments." Whatever their disagreements, both sides of this argument accept the idea that your basic moral choice is to be guided either by faith or by feelings. In other words, both sides agree that your choice is: religion or subjectivism. But if you want to live and enjoy life, neither of these will do. Neither religion nor subjectivism provides proper guidance for human action; each calls for human sacrifice and leads to human suffering—both physical and spiritual. To see why, we will look first at the theoretical essence of each of these doctrines; then we will turn to the practical consequences—historical and personal—of accepting them.

Let us begin with religion.

Religion holds that there is a God who demands your faith and obedience. He is said to be an all-powerful, all-knowing, all-good being who is the creator of the universe, the source of all truth, and the maker of moral law. Religion's basic moral tenet is: Don't place your self, your personal values, your own interests, your will, above those of God. Rather, you should live to glorify Him, to obey His commands, to fulfill His higher purpose. To do

3

otherwise—to act on behalf of your own selfish concerns as if your life were an end in itself—is to "sin." As the religious scholar Reverend John Stott declares: "God's order is that we put him first, others next, self last. Sin is the reversal of the order."[1]

According to religion, being moral consists not in pursuing your own interests, but in self-sacrificially serving God. Theologian and rabbi Abraham Heschel expresses this tenet as follows: "The essence and greatness of man do not lie in his ability to please his ego, to satisfy his needs, but rather in his ability to stand above his ego, to ignore his own needs; to sacrifice his own interests for the sake of the holy."[2]

Now, you might argue that to ignore your own needs and sacrifice your own interests is contrary to the requirements of your life and happiness. But according to religion, that is no ground for complaint, because, as theologian Walter Kaiser puts it: "God has the right to require human sacrifice."[3]

Disturbed by such an assertion, you might ask: What about God's love for man? If God loves us, why would he call for us to sacrifice? To which Dr. Stott answers: "Self-sacrifice is what the Bible means by 'love.'"[4]

Taking yet another angle, you might argue that self-sacrifice leads to suffering. But this fact is no ground for complaint either, because, according to the Bible, Adam disobeyed God by eating some forbidden fruit; therefore, you and I and all of Adam's descendents *deserve* to suffer.[5] As Saint Augustine put it: "We are suffering the just retribution of the omnipotent God. It is because it was to Him that we [by way of Adam] refused our obedience and our service that our body, which used to be obedient, now troubles us by its insubordination."[6]

---

1. John R.W. Stott, *Basic Christianity* (London: InterVarsity Press, 1971), p. 78.
2. Abraham Heschel, *God in Search of Man, A Philosophy of Judaism* (New York: Farrar, Straus and Giroux, 1983), p. 117.
3. Walter C. Kaiser Jr. et al., *Hard Sayings of the Bible* (Illinois: InterVarsity Press, 1996), p. 127.
4. Stott, *Basic Christianity,* p. 79.
5. See Genesis, 2–3.
6. Saint Augustine, *City of God,* trans. Gerald G. Walsh et al. (New York: Doubleday, 1958), p. 314.

The "insubordination" to which Augustine refers has to do with the aversion many people have to ignoring their own needs and sacrificing their own interests. After all, self-sacrifice can be extremely painful, both physically and spiritually. It can even be fatal. But, according to religion, if God tells a person to do something, the person is morally obligated to do it—regardless of the difficulties or consequences involved.

For a biblical example of what such obedience can mean in practice, consider the case of Abraham and Isaac. According to the story, God told Abraham: "Take your son, your only son Isaac, whom you love, and go to the land of Moriah, and sacrifice him there as a burnt offering."[7] Needless to say, it would be very painful for a man to kill his son, whom he loves. Nevertheless, because Abraham was faithfully committed to obeying the will of God, he set out to do just that.

Was Abraham's choice moral? Should he have done it? Would *you* do it? What do religionists say about this? According to Saint Augustine: "The obedience of Abraham is rightly regarded as *magnificent* precisely because the killing of his son was a command so difficult to obey. . . ."[8]

Magnificent?

As shocking as Augustine's position may be, it is the only stance a dedicated religionist can take on the issue, because the only alternative is to challenge the alleged authority of God, and that is the cardinal religious no-no. "Above all," writes the devoutly religious René Descartes, reminding us of the applicable tenet, "we ought to submit to the Divine authority rather than to our own judgment even though the light of reason may seem to us to suggest, with the utmost clearness and evidence, something opposite."[9]

According to religion, God's will, however objectionable, is by definition good; and human judgment to the contrary, however rational, is by definition bad. The "real distinction between right

---

7. Genesis, 22:2.
8. Augustine, *City of God,* p. 313, emphasis added.
9. *The Philosophical Works of Descartes,* trans. Elizabeth S. Haldane and G.R.T. Ross (London: Cambridge University Press, 1973), Vol. I, p. 253.

and wrong," explains Bishop Robert Mortimer, "is independent of what we happen to think. It is rooted in the nature and will of God."

> When a man's conscience tells him that a thing is right, which is in fact what God wills, his conscience is true and its judgment correct; when a man's conscience tells him a thing is right which is, in fact, contrary to God's will, his conscience is false and telling him a lie.[10]

Thus, if God wills that a man should kill his son, then, regardless of what the man thinks, he should do it.

But, you might ask, isn't human sacrifice wrong *on principle?* Not according to religion. As Dr. Kaiser reminds us, the religious point of view is precisely that "human sacrifice cannot be condemned on principle. The truth is that God owns all life and has a right to give or take it as he wills. To reject on all grounds God's legitimate right to ask for life under any conditions would be to remove his sovereignty and question his justice. . . ."[11] Bishop Mortimer elaborates the religious position as follows:

> [God] has an absolute claim on our obedience. We do not exist in our own right, but only as His creatures, who ought therefore to do and be what He desires. We do not possess anything in the world, absolutely, not even our own bodies; we hold things in trust for God, who created them, and are bound, therefore, to use them only as He intends that they should be used.[12]

In short, the basic moral tenet of religion is that obedience to God must be *absolute*—calls for human sacrifice and all.

Granted, religion does not call for everyone to murder his child. But it does call for everyone to sacrifice his judgment and interests for the sake of an alleged God; and in order to uphold

---

10. Robert C. Mortimer, *Christian Ethics* (London: Hutchinson's University Library, 1950), p. 8.
11. Kaiser, *Hard Sayings of the Bible,* p. 126.
12. Mortimer, *Christian Ethics,* pp. 7–8.

this tenet *consistently,* a person must be willing to do just that. If he claims to accept the moral tenets of religion but fails to uphold them consistently, then, on his own terms, he is guilty of "sin"— and on anyone's terms, he is guilty of hypocrisy (the consequences of which we will get to shortly).

Given the sacrificial nature of religion, it is not surprising that many people reject it and embrace its alleged opposite: subjectivism. But if human sacrifice is the problem, subjectivism is no solution.

Whereas religion holds that God creates truth and moral law, subjectivism holds that *people* do; it is the view that truth and morality are not objective, but "subjective"—not discovered by the human mind, but *created* by it. This creed comes in several varieties, two of which are: personal subjectivism and social subjectivism.

Personal subjectivism is the idea that truth and morality are creations of the mind of the individual—or matters of personal opinion. *Social subjectivism* is the notion that truth and morality are creations of the mind of a collective (a group of people)—or matters of social convention. Personal subjectivism has been around for thousands of years; its father was Protagoras of ancient Greece.[13] Social subjectivism was born in the late eighteenth century; its father was the German philosopher Immanuel Kant.[14]

These two versions of subjectivism have been accepted over the years in varying degrees and with numerous twists. What is important for our present purpose is that, in some form or another, the notion that people create (rather than discover) truth and morality has been prevalent among intellectuals for almost a century. As sociologist Michael Schudson notes: "From the 1920s on, the idea that human beings individually and collectively construct the

13. See *Ancilla to the Pre-Socratic Philosophers,* trans. Kathleen Freeman (Cambridge: Harvard University Press, 1996), p. 125; and Wilhelm Windelband, *A History of Philosophy* (New York: Harper & Row, 1958), Vol. I, pp. 91–94.
14. See Immanuel Kant, *Critique of Pure Reason,* trans. Norman Kemp Smith (New York: St. Martin's Press, 1929), esp. pp. 22–25; *Prolegomena,* trans. Paul Carus (Chicago: Open Court, 1997), esp. pp. 79–84; and *Groundwork of the Metaphysics of Morals,* trans. Mary Gregor (New York: Cambridge University Press, 1997), esp. pp. 40–41, 58–59.

reality they deal with has held a central position in social thought."[15] And the dominant views on morality have been shaped accordingly. Let us look first at the ethics of social subjectivism.

Social subjectivism holds that truth and morality are matters of social convention. As Stanford professor Richard Rorty puts it: "There's no court of appeal higher than a democratic consensus."[16] In other words: The will of the majority determines what's true and what's right.[17] Social subjectivism's basic moral tenet is: Don't place your self, your independent judgment, your personal values, your selfish concerns, above those of the group or the "common good." Rather, you should subordinate your own thoughts and interests to the beliefs, needs, and desires of the "whole"—of which you are merely a "part."

On this view, being moral consists in pursuing not your own well-being and happiness, but the "greater" well-being and happiness of the group or collective. Your life is not an end in itself, but a means to the ends of society; thus, you should make personal sacrifices for society's "greater good." To do otherwise—to pursue your own selfish goals in disregard of the "collective will"—is to be immoral.

Note that the moral common denominator of religion and social subjectivism is *altruism:* the theory that being moral consists in self-sacrificially serving others. (*Alter* is Latin for *other;* "altruism" literally means "other-ism.") According to altruism, self-sacrifice for the sake of others is the standard of morality. Thus, as philosophy professor Louis Pojman acknowledges, "complete altruism" means "total self-effacement for the sake of others."[18] While the general theory does not specify which particular others

---

15. Michael Schudson, *Discovering the News* (New York: Basic Books, 1978), p. 6.
16. Richard Rorty, "The Next Left," interview by Scott Stossel, *Atlantic Unbound,* April 23, 1998.
17. Cf. Richard Rorty, *Objectivity, Relativism, and Truth* (New York: Cambridge University Press, 1991), esp. pp. 13–14, 21–22, 29; and *Achieving our Country: Leftist Thought in Twentieth-Century America* (Cambridge: Harvard University Press, 1998), pp. 27–29, 34–35.
18. Louis P. Pojman, *Ethics: Discovering Right and Wrong,* 3rd ed. (Belmont: Wadsworth, 1999), p. 78.

you should sacrifice for, both religion and social subjectivism are quick to fill in the blank: Religion says the significant other is "God"; social subjectivism says it is "society." Religion says you should sacrifice for the sake of the "holy"; social subjectivism says you should sacrifice for the sake of the "whole."

In one form or another, altruism is the generally accepted and propagated morality today. By and large, people equate "doing the right thing" with "selflessly doing things for others." Mother Teresa and Peace Corps types are regarded as paragons of virtue; selflessness is considered the mark of morality.

For a homey example of the ethics of social subjectivism, consider the widespread "volunteerism" or "community service" crusade. Presidents Clinton, Carter, Ford, Bush Sr., Bush Jr., General Colin Powell, Oprah Winfrey, Nancy Reagan, Alan Keyes, William F. Buckley, and so on—liberals, moderates, and conservatives alike—have all joined hands to advocate this so-called ideal. Why? What brings this unlikely crew together? The mutually accepted and unchallenged premise that people have a moral duty to serve others.

"Citizen service is the main way we recognize that we are responsible for one another," says Clinton.[19] Bush Sr. trumpets "an ethic of community service" and rhapsodizes about solving "pressing human problems" by means of "a vast galaxy of people working voluntarily in their own backyards."[20] Bush Jr. tells us that "Where there is suffering, there is duty" and that "Americans are generous and strong and decent, not because we believe in ourselves, but because we hold beliefs beyond ourselves"; thus, he asks us "to seek a common good beyond our comfort" and "to serve our nation" by "building communities of service."[21]

Keyes, Buckley, and their ilk advocate *mandatory* service. Keyes claims that "citizenship in the end is about understanding that each and every individual must offer and must participate in the national life"; thus, he wants to establish a system in which

---

19. President Bill Clinton, radio address to the nation, April 5, 1997.
20. President George Bush, quoted in Howard Radest, *Community Service: Encounter with Strangers* (Westport: Praeger, 1993), p. 8.
21. President George W. Bush, inaugural address, January 20, 2001.

"people are thrown together to live for a couple of years a common life of service."[22] Extending the mandatory-service agenda to the realm of business, Buckley calls for "a national corporate commitment to public service," acknowledging: "I sound like a goddamned socialist!"[23] Which brings us back to Clinton, who, applying the same idea to the realm of education, urges "every state to make service a part of the curriculum in high school or even in middle school," adding: "There are many creative ways to do this— including giving students credit for service, incorporating service into course work, putting service on a student's transcript, or even *requiring* service as a condition of graduation, as Maryland does." (In 1993, Maryland became the first state in America to require community service as a condition of high school graduation. Since then, hundreds of school districts nationwide have followed suit.) Why? Because, says Clinton: "Every young American should be taught the joy and the duty of serving, and should learn it at the moment when it will have the most enduring impact on the rest of their lives."[24] General Powell chimes in, admonishing young people: "Listen, you're going to be a real citizen in this country; you have to serve; you have to do something in service to your community." How? Powell tells them: "By tutoring younger children or working at a hospice or homeless center."[25] And so forth.

But, one might ask, what about individual rights? What about the basic principle of America? How does mandatory service reconcile with the right to life, liberty, and the pursuit of happiness? And what about a child's education? What about his future? Shouldn't he be learning math, science, English, and history during school hours— *not* "volunteering" or being forced to serve the homeless?

Powell's answer: "If you want to know what violated my rights, it was integral calculus, not community service."[26]

---

22. Alan Keyes, *Washington Journal,* C-SPAN, January 19, 2000.
23. William F. Buckley, quoted in *Mother Jones,* January/February, 1996.
24. President Bill Clinton, radio addresses to the nation, April 5 and July 26, 1997, emphasis added.
25. General Colin Powell, "Helping Hands," interview by Elizabeth Farnsworth, *Jim Lehrer News Hour,* April 28, 1997.
26. Ibid.

So, teaching a child math is a violation of his rights, but forcing him to empty a stranger's bedpan is not? Surely the General is joking. As to the reason for his sarcasm, we will get to that later.

The point here is that the goal of the "community service" crusade is to spread the idea that in order to be "moral" one must be altruistic—one must selflessly serve others.

Given the self-sacrificial nature of altruism, it is not surprising that some people reject it altogether—in both its religious and its social forms. But the rejection of a negative is not the adoption of a positive. And in the absence of a *rational* replacement, the only alternative to altruism is the so-called "selfishness" of personal subjectivism.

Personal subjectivism is the view that truth and morality are matters of personal opinion. Its slogans are: "What's true for you may not be true for me" and "Who's to say what's right?" Its basic moral tenet is: Do whatever you *feel* like doing. In other words: There's no such thing as morality.

On this view, values are entirely a function of personal feelings. As the British philosopher Bertrand Russell puts it: "When we assert that this or that has 'value,' we are giving expression to our own emotions, not to a fact which would still be true if our personal feelings were different."[27]

Accordingly, a personal subjectivist values whatever he *feels* like valuing; he acts however he *feels* like acting. If he feels like sacrificing other people, he does so. He is not concerned with individual rights; he cares only about his feelings. Since he feels that he creates his own morality, he feels that he is entitled to place his feelings above all else—including the rights of others (which he may or may not feel that they have). This mentality is demonstrated by criminals who, when asked why they committed such-and-such a crime, reply in so many words: "Because I felt like it."

---

27. Bertrand Russell, "Science and Ethics," in *Religion and Science* (New York: Oxford University Press, 1997), pp. 230–31.

The most common form of personal subjectivism is *hedonism:* the theory that being moral consists in acting in whatever manner gives you pleasure. (*Hedone* is Greek for *pleasure;* "hedonism" means "pleasure-ism.") According to hedonism, pleasure is the standard of morality. And while "pleasure" may sound less subjective than "feeling" as the standard, in practice the two are the same. Morally speaking, "Because it gives me pleasure" means "Because I feel like it." Hedonism is just glorified personal subjectivism.

A textbook example of a personal subjectivist is Eric Harris, one of the murderers of twelve students and a teacher at Columbine High School (Littleton, Colorado, 1999). Prior to the massacre, Harris had expressed his philosophy in no uncertain terms: "My belief is that if I say something, it goes. I am the law, and if you don't like it, you die. If I don't like you or I don't like what you want me to do, you die."[28] He acted on that very belief.

Such ideas are horrifying. If we want to live as civilized beings, we need a code of moral principles to guide us not only in living our own lives, but also in recognizing the rights of others to live theirs. We need a code of values by reference to which we can say with moral certainty that some choices and actions are absolutely right and others are absolutely wrong.

This is one reason why, despite the sacrifices it requires, many people turn to religion: God is widely believed to be the only possible source of an absolute morality. This view is expressed succinctly in a popular book titled *The Ten Commandments,* by Dr. Laura Schlessinger and Rabbi Stewart Vogel:

> To believe in God is to believe that humans are more than accidents of nature. It means that we are endowed with purpose by a higher source, and that our goal is to realize that higher purpose. If each of us creates his own meaning, we also create our own morality. I cannot believe this. For if so, what the Nazis did was not immoral because German society had accepted it. Likewise, the subjective morality of every majority culture

---

28. Eric Harris, from his website, quoted in *The Washington Post,* April 29, 1999.

throughout the world could validate their heinous behavior. It comes down to a very simple matter: Without God there is no *objective meaning* to life, nor is there an *objective morality*. I do not want to live in a world where right and wrong are subjective.[29]

I don't want to live in such a world either. And an objective morality is precisely what is needed. But the question remains: Does religion provide it? Is a God-based morality really objective? If not, it is no antidote to subjectivism.

"Objective" means "fact-based." For morality to be objective, it has to be based on a standard of value derived not from feelings, but from facts. Convinced that no such standard can be found here in the *natural* world—and justifiably horrified by what is believed to be the only alternative (subjectivism)—many people turn to the *supernatural,* to God, in hopes of filling the moral void. And God is believed to solve the problem. On the premise that He is the creator of all things and the source of all truth, His moral authority is *absolute.* Thus, being good is pretty straightforward: Simply obey God's commands—whatever they are—and the problem is solved.

Until you think about it.

There are hundreds of religions. Each is vying for your allegiance. Each denies the validity of the others. Each claims to be based on the "true" word of God. And each says that God said something different from what the others say He said.

Why? Why can't any single religion convince the others of its divine "truth"? Because none can provide rational *evidence* in support of its particular assertions. And given the religious method of arriving at the "truth," none can justify demanding such evidence from the others either.

Religion is based explicitly, not on reason, which requires evidence and logic, but on *faith,* which is acceptance of ideas in the absence of evidence and in defiance of logic.[30] Faith is *essential* to religion, because it is the only way to maintain belief in the existence of God: There is no evidence for Him; there are only books and

---

29. Dr. Laura Schlessinger and Rabbi Stewart Vogel, *The Ten Commandments* (New York: Harper Collins, 1998), p. xxix.

30. Cf. Hebrews, 11:1; and Heschel, *God in Search of Man,* pp. 117–18.

people that *say* He exists. (This fact can be verified by asking any religionist to present the evidence on which his belief in God rests.)

How, then, do religionists attempt to justify their belief in God? By insisting, as does Dr. Laura, that God is "not an aspect of nature but a reality greater than the universe" and "beyond our sensory abilities."[31]

But that raises the question: How can anyone know anything about that which is "not an aspect of nature" or "greater than the universe" or "beyond our sensory abilities"? Nature is *all* there is; the universe is the *totality* of it; and our senses are our *only* source of information. In other words, such "knowledge" would require understanding of a *non*-thing from a *non*-place by means of *non*-sense.

This is why religionists of all walks ultimately echo the famous words of Saint Augustine: I do not know in order to believe; I believe in order to know.[32]

By dismissing the requirement of evidence—and thus reversing the order of knowledge and belief—faith sets the stage for belief in "miracles." A miracle is (supposedly) when something becomes what it has no natural potential to become (water turns into wine, or a woman into a pillar of salt)—or when something acts in a manner in which it has no natural potential to act (a bush speaks or burns without being consumed). In other words, a miracle is a violation of the laws of nature.

The basic laws of nature are the laws of identity and causality. The *law of identity* is the self-evident truth that everything is something specific; everything has properties that make it what it is; everything has a nature: A thing is what it is. (A rose is a rose.) The *law of causality* is the law of identity applied to action: A thing can act only in accordance with its nature.[33] (A rose can bloom; it cannot speak.)

---

31. Schlessinger, *The Ten Commandments,* pp. 25–26.
32. Cf. Saint Augustine, "Tractate 27 on the Gospel of John," Chapter 6: 60–72. Cf. also Saint Anselm, *Proslogium,* Chapter 1; and Heschel, *God in Search of Man,* pp. 121–22.
33. See Ayn Rand, *For the New Intellectual* (New York: Signet, 1963), p. 151; and H.W.B. Joseph, *Introduction to Logic,* 2nd ed. (Oxford: Clarendon Press, 1916), p. 408.

Insofar as our thinking is in accordance with the laws of identity and causality, our thinking is in accordance with reality; insofar as it is not, it is not. Our method for checking our ideas against the facts is *logic:* the method of non-contradictory identification.[34]

The basic law of logic is the *law of non-contradiction,* which is the law of identity in negative form: A thing cannot be both what it is and what it is not at the same time and in the same respect.[35] (A rose cannot simultaneously be a non-rose.) The law of non-contradiction is the basic principle of rational thinking. Since a contradiction cannot exist in nature—since things are what they are—if a contradiction exists in our thinking, then our thinking is mistaken and in need of correction. (If we believe that a bush spoke or burned without being consumed, then we need to correct our thinking.)

The laws of identity, causality, and non-contradiction are not rationally debatable. To begin with, all arguments presuppose and depend on their validity; any attempt to deny them actually reaffirms them. This phenomenon was first discovered by Aristotle and is called *reaffirmation through denial.* While trying to deny these laws, a person has to be who he is—he can't be someone else—because of the law of identity; he has to act as a human being—he can't act as an eggplant—because of the law of causality; and he has to use words that mean what they mean—he can't use words that mean what they don't—because of the law of non-contradiction. On a more practical level, these laws are why we fuel our cars with gasoline—why we refrigerate certain foods—why we wear warm clothing in winter—why we vaccinate our children—why we string our tennis rackets—why we put wings on airplanes—and why we don't drink Drano. More broadly speaking, the entire history of observation, knowledge, and science is based on the laws of identity, causality, and non-contradiction. Every object, every event, every discovery, and every utterance is an example of their validity. These laws are self-evident, immutable, and absolute.

---

34. Rand, *For the New Intellectual,* p. 126.
35. Cf. Aristotle, "Metaphysics," in *The Basic Works of Aristotle,* ed. Richard McKeon (New York: Random House, 1941), pp. 736–37.

Yet religion flatly denies them.

Different religions go to different lengths in this regard, but all of them deny natural law and logic. Such denial is *essential* to religion, because if a thing cannot become what it has no natural potential to become, or act in a manner contrary to its nature, then there can be no miracles. In other words, if natural law is immutable, then there can be no omnipotent God capable of overriding, suspending, or muting it.

Thus, the more religious a person is, the more he has to try to defend contradictions. Such an effort is by nature frustrating, because contradictions are by nature indefensible. This is why the staunchest defenders of religion say the nuttiest things. For instance, while responding to criticisms of the illogic of religious dogma, the outspoken church father Tertullian finally declared: "It is by all means to be believed, because it is absurd. . . . The fact is certain, because it is impossible."[36]

According to religion, God's existence and mysterious ways are incomprehensible to reason—which means they don't make sense. God is purported to be greater than nature and unrestrained by natural law—which is what "supernatural" means. Hence, His existence and authority cannot be proved but must be accepted on faith—that is, in the absence of evidence and in defiance of logic. "To those who have faith," the argument goes, "no explanation is necessary; to those who do not, no explanation is possible."

This is how an argument for God always ends. One believes *because* one believes—which means: because one *wants* to. Religion is a doctrine based not on facts, but on *feelings*. Thus, claims to the contrary notwithstanding, *religion is a form of subjectivism.*

In light of this fact, it should come as no surprise that while *secular* subjectivism denies some of religion's unproved, evidence-free claims, it demands and employs the very same methods—faith, mysticism, and dogma.

For instance, according to the Nazis, Hitler's will determined the truth. As expressed by the commander in chief of the Nazi air force, Hermann Goering: "If the Fuhrer wishes it then two times

---

36. *The Ante-Nicene Fathers,* eds. A. Roberts and J. Donaldson (New York: Charles Scribner's Sons, 1903), Vol. III, The Writings of Tertullian, p. 525.

two are five."[37] Goering elaborated the Nazi position as follows in his book titled *Germany Reborn.*

> Just as the Roman Catholic considers the Pope infallible in all matters concerning religion and morals, so do we National Socialists believe with the same inner conviction that for us the Leader is in all political and other matters concerning the national and social interests of the people simply infallible. Wherein lies the secret of this enormous influence which he [Hitler] has on his followers? ... It is something mystical, inexpressible, almost incomprehensible which this unique man possesses, and he who cannot feel it instinctively will not be able to grasp it at all.[38]

According to the Nazis, to *feel* Hitler's mystical authority and infallibility is to know it—and feeling it is the *only* way to know it. In other words: "To those who feel it, no explanation is necessary; to those who do not, no explanation is possible."

Exactly.

The subjectivism feared by religionists is a product of the very method demanded by religion. The Nazis relied on faith as their primary ally in the campaign to convince people of Hitler's divine authority and the superiority of the "master race." They could not offer any evidence in support of these things—because none exists. They could not offer logical arguments in support of them—because none are possible. But they could demand belief in the absence of evidence and in defiance of logic—and that is what they did.

Now, of what *practical* use was faith to the Nazis? What was it that they desperately wanted people to do, but could not rationally persuade them to do? The appeal to faith was the Nazi means of convincing people that they had a moral duty to ignore all personal concerns in favor of serving the group. In *Mein Kampf,*

---

37. Quoted in Eugene Davidson, *The Trial of the Germans* (New York: Macmillan, 1966), pp. 237–38.
38. Hermann Goering, *Germany Reborn* (London: E. Mathews and Marrot, 1934), pp. 79–80.

Hitler wrote that the individual must "renounce putting forward his personal opinion and interests and sacrifice both. . . ."

> This state of mind, which subordinates the interests of the ego to the conservation of the community, is really the first premise for every truly human culture. . . . The basic attitude from which such activity arises, we call—to distinguish it from egoism and selfishness—idealism. By this we understand only the individual's capacity to make sacrifices for the community, for his fellow men.[39]

Sound familiar?

The Nazis harnessed people's willingness to "just believe." Combining religious mysticism and secular subjectivism, they were able to gain adherents without a shred of evidence in support of their claims. Hitler's alleged God-like will was purported to be the standard of truth. "The community" was put forth as the highest value. "The individual's capacity to make sacrifices" was trumpeted as the greatest virtue. The subordination of the individual to society was said to be the essence of a "truly human culture." The people did not challenge this. They did not ask for evidence. They did not use logic. They simply had faith. In Augustinian terms: They first believed in order that they could then know.

Observe the pattern here. Posing as representatives of an alleged God's all-powerful, all-knowing, all-benevolent will, religious leaders convince people of a moral duty to sacrifice selflessly in service of God's "higher purpose." On behalf of Hitler's allegedly omnipotent and infallible will, and toward a so-called "truly human culture," Nazi leaders convinced people of a moral duty to sacrifice selflessly in service of their "fellow men" or the "master race" (depending on whether or not they were "Aryan"). In the name of the "proletariat," and toward an anti-individual "utopia" of collectivism, communist leaders convince people of a moral duty to sacrifice selflessly in service of the "community" (hence the name communism). In the name of "compassion," and

---

39. Adolf Hitler, *Mein Kampf*, trans. Ralph Manheim (Houghton Mifflin: New York, 1971), pp. 297–98.

toward the so-called "common good," America's advocates of so-cial subjectivism convince people of a moral duty to sacrifice self-lessly in service of the "politically correct" group *du jour*—the "race," the "class," the "gender," the "homeless," the "community," the "nation," or simply "society." And snarling, "I am the law" and "If I say something, it goes," personal subjectivists convince themselves of their "right" to sacrifice whomever they want to sacrifice.

Now observe what is being argued. Religion claims that every-one should sacrifice himself and that the beneficiary should be "God." Social subjectivism claims that everyone should sacrifice himself and that the beneficiary should be "society." And personal subjectivism claims that others should sacrifice themselves and that the beneficiary should be "me." Each form of subjectivism calls for human sacrifice; the debate is merely over who should sacrifice for the sake of whom.

Finally, observe the evidence offered in support of their claims: zero.

In light of this fact, shouldn't we ask: Why should anyone sacrifice or be sacrificed for the sake of anyone? What good is hu-man sacrifice? What, other than suffering and death, does it ac-complish? And if there is no good reason for human sacrifice, shouldn't people stop advocating it? Shouldn't we abandon and condemn any moral code that requires, encourages, or permits it?

In case there are any doubts, history provides conclusive evi-dence of the sacrificial nature of all three forms of subjectivism. Let us look first at religion.

Countless people have suffered and died in the name of God. Here is just a smattering of the carnage and pain perpetrated on His "behalf." The Middle Ages were ten continuous centuries fraught with misery and bloodshed in obedience to God's "merci-ful will." During the Crusades, tens of thousands of men, women, and children were massacred for God's "higher purpose." From the thirteenth through the eighteenth century, the Inquisition rou-tinely branded people as "heretics," and then imprisoned, tortured, hanged, or burned them at the stake for the "love" of God. (Vic-tims include the courageous astronomer Giordano Bruno, who was burned alive for the "heresy" of thinking—and the great scientist

Galileo, who was sentenced to life under house arrest for defying the Church by reporting the truth.) The Thirty Years' War was, well, thirty uninterrupted years of Protestants and Catholics slaughtering each other over how best to worship the Almighty. (This feud resumed in twentieth-century Northern Ireland and has continued for an additional forty years—and counting.) In seventeenth-century Massachusetts, Christians held "witch" trials and hanged or crushed to death those whom they *felt* were "guilty." Before moving on to his "next life," the Ayatollah Khomeini issued an Islamic *fatwa* (a religious decree) against author Salman Rushdie—who is to be executed for "insulting" Allah in his novel *The Satanic Verses.* In Afghanistan, throughout the turn of the century, the Islamic Taliban regularly beat, jailed, and murdered people for breaking Allah's laws. (The punished include: women for holding a job or exposing their ankles, men for failing to wear a beard, homosexuals for existing, and anyone for partaking in activities such as playing music, dancing, playing soccer, playing cards, taking photographs, or flying a kite.) In 1998, terrorist Osama bin Laden and his Muslim cohorts issued a *fatwa* declaring: "To kill the Americans and their allies, civilians and military, is an individual duty for every Muslim who can do it in any country in which it is possible to do it." This, they said, "is in accordance with the words of Almighty God."[40] Such faithful terrorists ceaselessly plot and occasionally strike against "the Great Satan" America by such means as hijacking commercial airliners and crashing them into skyscrapers full of people. In the Middle East, the so-called "Holy Land" over which Islamic terrorists regularly spill Jewish blood has not seen peace since religion began. Religious disputes between Eastern Orthodox Christians, Roman Catholics, and Muslims are at the core of centuries of hatred and the ongoing bloodbath in the Balkans. And in America, anti-abortionists shoot doctors dead for tampering with God's "divine plan" and bomb abortion clinics because women dare to assume that they, rather than God, own their bodies.

Of course, each religion and sect denounces the others and objects to their ways, calling them "aberrations," "fringe fanatics,"

---

40. Osama bin Laden et al., "Fatwa Urging Jihad Against Americans," in *Al-Quds al-'Arabi,* February 23, 1998.

"cultists," "extremists," "defects," "misinterpreters of God's will," or just plain "wrong." *But by what standard?* Each claims to get its morality by means of "revelation" from God; thus, each claims to have "divine" authority to act as it does. And since none can prove that its particular creed is right, none has any standard by which to show that the others are wrong. They all just *feel* it.

I could go on and on about the baseless and sacrificial nature of religion; instead, however, I will defer to Jean Meslier, a guilt-ridden priest who conceded the following in his last will and testament, titled *Common Sense:*

> We have seen, a thousand times, in all parts of our globe, infu-riated fanatics slaughtering each other, lighting the funeral piles, committing without scruple, as a matter of duty, the greatest crimes. Why? To maintain or to propagate the impertinent con-jectures of enthusiasts, or to sanction the knaveries of imposters on account of a being who exists only in their imagination.[41]

As Voltaire said: "If we believe in absurdities, we shall com-mit atrocities."

Amen.

Amazingly, social subjectivism has an even more horrifying and bloodier history than religion does—and over a much shorter period of time. In the twentieth century alone, over a hundred mil-lion people were sacrificed in the name of some group's "greater good." Various socialist regimes—communists, Nazis, and fas-cists—starved, tortured, and slaughtered men, women, and chil-dren for the sake of the "community" or "proletariat" or "race" or "peasants" or "farmers" or "nation" or some other collective. In each case, human sacrifice was considered a moral imperative and thus became a political policy. The atrocities perpetrated in the concentration camps of Nazi Germany, the purges and gulags of Soviet Russia, and the killing fields of communist Cambodia are too well known to warrant recital here. Suffice it to say that until the atrocities of Black Tuesday (September 11, 2001), the human

---

41. Jean Meslier, *Superstition in All Ages,* trans. Anna Knoop (New York: Peter Eckler, 1889) pp. 37–38.

sacrifice caused by social subjectivism made the human sacrifice caused by religion look comparatively humane.

Finally, there is personal subjectivism—the creed of common criminals, sundry lowlifes, and creatures of prey that sacrifice people because, well, they want to. This mentality is responsible for countless murders, rapes, muggings, robberies, and frauds. Read any newspaper for details.

It is painfully obvious that all three forms of subjectivism necessarily lead to physical conflict and destruction. What is also true, but not so obvious, is that each one necessarily leads to *spiritual* conflict and destruction—to conflicting ideas and emotions—to destruction of the mind. Again, let us take religion first.

To the extent a person is religious, he believes that he has a duty to self-sacrificially serve God. This duty requires him to abandon his own selfish dreams. If he sticks to his faithful convictions and abandons his dreams, he cannot be happy, because his dreams go forever unrealized. Conversely, if he hypocritically abandons his convictions and pursues his dreams, he still cannot be happy, for he is filled with moral guilt and dread of divine retribution.

Of course, few people take religion as seriously as did Abraham who, according to the Bible, was willing to murder his son in order to please God. And few are as dedicated as the medieval saints who, in order to avoid the sin of selfish pleasure, drank muddy water, sprinkled ashes on their food, used rocks for pillows, and flogged themselves for having sexual desires.[42] But the point is that to whatever degree a person does accept the idea that he should sacrifice his own interests for the sake of God, he will suffer: either from guilt and fear or from psychological repression—or both.   •

Consider a young woman who longs to become a great ballerina, but cannot reconcile such a purely self-interested goal with her religious conviction that she ought somehow to selflessly serve God. If she chooses to pursue her interest in dance, she cannot be happy, because she will feel guilty and live in fear. If she chooses

---

42. See W.E.H. Lecky, *History of European Morals* (New York: George Braziller, 1955), Vol. II, pp. 107–12; and St. Bonaventura, *Life of St. Francis,* trans. E.G. Slater (London: J.M. Dent and Sons, 1910), pp. 329–31.

to become a nun or a missionary, or to serve God in some other way, she still cannot be happy, since her personal dream will go forever unrealized. And if she compromises—if she pursues dance less seriously than is necessary to realize her full potential, and in the place of that surrendered portion of her dream she somehow serves God's "higher purpose"—then she will get exactly what you would expect: a compromised, semi-guilty, semi-repressed sort of happiness. For she could have either sacrificed more to "glorify" God or worked harder to achieve her dream. She could have been either more "moral" or more selfish.

Fortunately, adherence to religion is losing popularity. Unfortunately, in its stead, people are turning to the other forms of subjectivism.

Consciously or not, many people have accepted the ethics of social subjectivism. They believe that their own welfare and happiness are morally subordinate to the welfare and happiness of some group: a race, a class, a gender, a culture, a nation, or "others" in general. Taken straight, few people could swallow this notion. But it is rarely given straight. To make the sacrifice required by this creed more palatable, the altruistic pill is usually coated in hedonistic sugar and called "utilitarianism."

In his book titled *Utilitarianism,* the British philosopher John Stuart Mill writes: "The creed which accepts as the foundation of morals 'utility' or 'the greatest happiness principle' holds that actions are right in proportion as they tend to promote happiness; wrong as they tend to produce the reverse of happiness." Importantly, however:

> That standard is not the agent's *own* greatest happiness, but the greatest amount of happiness altogether; and if it may possibly be doubted whether a noble character is always the happier for its nobleness, there can be no doubt that it makes *other* people happier, and that the world in general is immensely a gainer by it.[43]

---

43. John Stuart Mill, *Utilitarianism* (Indianapolis: Hackett, 1979), pp. 7, 11, emphasis added. Cf. Immanuel Kant, *The Metaphysics of Morals,* trans. Mary Gregor (New York: Cambridge University Press, 1996), esp. pp. 151–52, 156, 161, 227.

Now, few people go so far as to ask themselves, "How can I act to make the whole world happy?" But, again, to the degree a person believes that he should selflessly serve others, his own happiness is thereby thwarted—one way or another.

Consider a young man who aspires to be a great classical pianist but cannot reconcile such a thoroughly self-interested career with his altruistic conviction that he is first and foremost a member of an ethnic group, and thus has a moral duty to live for "his people"—not for himself. Classical piano is not considered a part of the cultural heritage of "his people," and his pursuit of it would not contribute to their "needs." In fact, it would remove him from the community where most of them live; it would require that he leave them behind. If he chooses to pursue piano, he cannot be happy, because he will suffer from guilt and shame for abandoning his ethnic group. If, instead, he dutifully stays in his community and becomes a teacher, he still cannot be happy, for he will never hear the beautiful music he could have made. And if he compromises—if he pursues piano less seriously than his dream requires, and spends his "spare" time and energy performing some kind of community service—then the effect is predictable: a compromised, semi-guilty, semi-repressed sort of happiness. Like the dancer, he could have either sacrificed more to serve others or worked harder to achieve his dream. He could have been either more "moral" or more selfish.

The point is that if altruism is moral—if morality is a matter of self-sacrificially serving others—then morality is an impediment to your life and happiness: Being good is not good for you. Either life is a paradox in which it is neither practical to be moral nor moral to be practical, or self-interest is moral. It is one or the other.

Take another example. Consider a young girl who dreams of becoming a great physicist. Such a goal requires that she apply herself to her fullest potential in her studies. She must devote her time and effort to achieving the highest level of understanding possible; she has to earn her way into a top university; she needs to learn from the best minds in the field. She cannot compromise: If she does, she will not make it.

But suppose that one day a General, in his military uniform, visits the girl's school and tells her and her classmates, as he is fond of telling children: "Listen, you're going to be a real citizen in this country."

"What do you mean?" asks the wide-eyed, ambitious little girl.

"You have to serve," says the General, "you have to do something in service to your community."

"Would you be more specific, sir? What do you mean? Exactly how must I serve?" asks the active-minded, curious child.

"By tutoring younger children or working at a hospice or homeless center," says the General.

"But why?" asks the persistent and brave young girl. "Why should I serve others at the expense of my own dream? What about my studies? What about the fact that I want to be a great physicist, not a social worker? If I am to succeed, I need to become an expert at math and science, not at ladling soup. And what about the basic principle of America? Don't I have a right to my own life and the pursuit of my own happiness?"

"If you want to know what violated my rights," quips the General, "it was integral calculus, not community service."

Observe that the little girl has asked the General for a *reason*, but he has not given her one. She has asked him *why* she must serve others at the expense of her own dream, but he has not told her why. She has asked him to reconcile his position with the basic principle of America, but he has not done so. Instead, he has evaded her questions by resorting to sarcasm. Why? Why won't he give her a straight answer? *Because he can't.* There is no rational justification for what he says she must do; there is no rational justification for self-sacrifice.

There simply are no facts to support the claim that the little girl should spend some of her precious time and energy manning a ladle in a soup kitchen, or sponge bathing the elderly, or in some other way emulating Mother Teresa. The General can *say* that the little girl has to serve her community, but he cannot say *why* she has to do so. Hence his sarcasm: It is an attempt to avoid having to give a reason for his claim—a claim for which no reason can be given.

If the sarcasm doesn't work, if the little girl continues to demand a reason why she should self-sacrificially serve others, the

General might try appealing to an alleged authority—whether himself ("Because I said so") or some "higher" authority such as "God" or "society." And if that doesn't work, if the little girl rejects those fallacious appeals, the General might try appealing to force; he might try making the child serve others against her will (as his altruistic allies in Maryland do). But whatever he does, he cannot appeal to reason, because there is no reason why the little girl should serve others at the expense of her own dream.

What if the General succeeds? What if his sarcasm works? What if he artfully dodges the little girl's questions and badgers her into accepting the creed of self-sacrifice? To the extent she accepts it, like the dancer and the pianist, her life will be thwarted by moral guilt, compromise, and repression. What if the General appeals to authority and *that* works? What if he convinces the little girl that he or God or society just knows that she must sacrifice herself for others—but that no reason can be given, and that in order to understand, she must simply feel it or accept it on faith? Again, to the degree she accepts it, her life will be retarded by moral guilt, compromise, and repression. And what if the General appeals to force? What if (Maryland-style) he makes the little girl serve others against her will? To the extent he imposes such force on the child, her life will be impeded by, well, involuntary servitude—which, in principle, is slavery.

Whatever the means, if the General has his way, damage will be done. Every moment of life counts. Every amount of effort matters. Once time and energy are spent, they cannot be retrieved. Thus, if the little girl is convinced to sacrifice or forced to serve, she will not be able to make up her loss. That much of her dream will be out of her reach forever.

Now, what are we to make of an adult's efforts to coerce or convince a little girl to serve others at the expense of her own long-range goal in life? Bear in mind: We are not talking here about an adult trying to guide a child to act in her own long-term best interest—that is precisely what the little girl in question is trying to do. Rather, we are talking about an adult's attempt to thwart that process by persuading the child to put her time and effort elsewhere, by evading her questions as to why, by appealing to authority, or by using physical force.

I submit that for an adult to sacrifice himself is immoral—but for an adult to force or encourage the sacrifice of a child is *evil.*

People live once. Ideas have consequences. Human sacrifices are being encouraged and performed as you read. Altruism, in both its religious and its secular forms, is crippling the lives of real men, women, and children every day. You probably know some of them. You may be one of them. I was.

There is only one way to combat a morality that is *against* human life, and that is by embracing a morality that is *for* human life—a non-sacrificial morality—the morality of self-interest.

But, one might ask, doesn't self-interest imply personal subjectivism? Don't selfish people do whatever they feel like doing? Don't they harm others for their own benefit? And how can an advocate of selfishness say that sacrificing other people is wrong?

To begin answering these questions, let us observe the so-called "selfishness" of a personal subjectivist. He, too, has dreams—and he feels that he can "achieve" them in whatever fashion he wants to. If he feels like sacrificing other people—so be it! According to his philosophy, he is the law; thus, he makes up the rules as he goes.

Consider a hedonist who wants the pleasures that money can bring but doesn't feel like being productive. Working, he says, is just not his thing. So he decides to steal pocketbooks—they can be full of cash and are relatively easy to snatch. Sure enough, with a few select purses a day, the money starts to flow, and he feels that he is on his way to achieving his dream. In just a few months, he has stolen thousands of dollars and has moved into a fashionably furnished big-city apartment.

But for some reason, he still feels empty. His friends lie and try to steal from him; surprisingly, they, too, are crooks. He can't seem to keep the attention of any quality women; they all want to talk about career goals, achievements, and ambitions. The party scene has gotten old; there is really nothing to celebrate. Of course, the money is still "good," and the routine has become even easier with repetition. But somehow life just seems meaningless.

So he decides to rob a bank. He figures that if he can pull off one big "job" and make it to the islands with a million dollars in his suitcase, he will never have another discouraging day. He begins to plan the heist. "Selfish" bliss is just over the horizon. . .

Or is it?

What if he makes it? Some criminals have. What will he do on the island? Go scuba diving? Watch TV? Get drunk? "Hang out" with other criminals? Pretend that he is a man of virtue in order to associate with good people to whom he has lied? Who will be his lover? Will she be intelligent, passionate, and have good character? Or will she be ignorant, boring, and likely to steal his stolen money? How will he sleep at night? How will he feel when he wakes up in the morning? How will he face each day? Will he be fearless and eager to meet his next challenge? Or will he be timid and terrified that the law might catch up with him? What will be his *true* inner state? Will it be one of harmony—or one of anxiety?

The point is: It doesn't matter if he makes it. He can't possibly achieve happiness by his chosen method. If asked, he might swear up and down that his is a life of pure pleasure. But so what? Words cannot reverse cause and effect. Words cannot change the fact that genuine happiness can be achieved only by means of honest effort. And while even a bank robber probably knows this on some level, even if he doesn't, his ignorance is not bliss. His is a life of emptiness, self-contempt, loneliness, and decay. Emptiness, because he has no rational ambitions or productive goals. Self-contempt, because he knows that he is a parasite. Loneliness, because he is incapable and undeserving of friendship or love. And decay, because he does not use his mind, and there is no such thing as a dormant mind: One that does not grow, rots. Such a person is rotting spiritually from the inside out.

Of course, few people are as brazenly irrational as is our hedonist bank robber. But irrationality of any kind or degree is incompatible with genuine happiness: The psychological results vary in proportion to the extent of one's subjectivism. To the extent a person allows irrational desires to dictate his choices and actions, he *will* be unhappy. To the degree he does whatever he feels like doing without regard to both the short-range and the long-range consequences—including both the physical and the spiritual effects—he *will* suffer.

For example, a businessman who "just occasionally" swindles his way through a deal thereby ruins his potential for genuine happiness. He might have wads of money, a big summerhouse, a trophy wife, a yacht, and lots of so-called friends, but he still cannot be happy. Not if happiness requires harmony with reality: By pretending that facts are other than they are, he has set himself in conflict with reality. And not if happiness requires self-respect: He has been dishonest—and he knows it. In addition to the fact that he is a fraud and might get exposed to the world as such, even if he doesn't get physically "caught," the swindler still has major self-imposed problems. Either he lies to his so-called friends about the nature of his success, in which case they are not friends—or he doesn't, in which case they are swine, too. His wife would hate him if she knew him—or worse, she would not. And though he may be too blind to see it, or too belligerent to admit it, he is not happy. Neither ignorance, nor insistence, nor more fraud can change that fact.

Regardless of what they might say, personal subjectivists are miserable people, and they are so by their own design. Yet they are typically considered "selfish." Is that an appropriate label for them? Does it make any sense to call a person "selfish" for extinguishing the very possibility of his own happiness? Not if selfishness means concern for one's own well-being. Spiritual self-destruction is no more in a person's best interest than is physical self-destruction; we would not call a person selfish for mutilating his own hand, and we should not call him selfish for mangling his own mind.

Neither bloody murderers, nor big-time bank robbers, nor small-time purse-snatchers, nor occasional swindlers are selfish—not in the true meaning of the term. And it is no coincidence that none of them are happy. Blindly following one's feelings—evading, ignoring, or denying the requirements of one's actual, long-term well-being—is not in one's best interest. Irrationality is not selfish; it is self*less.*

For a policy to be selfish, it has to account for one's actual nature and needs—both material and spiritual; and it has to account not only for the present, but also for the more distant future. A policy of self-interest must recognize the fact that man is a being of body and mind whose life occurs not for just a moment or a day, but for a span of years and decades.

If being selfish were a matter of acting on one's feelings, it would not be conducive to happiness. But it *isn't* a matter of acting on one's feelings. As we will see, being selfish consists in thinking logically and acting on long-range principles toward life-serving goals—both material and spiritual. Being selfish consists in being *rational.*

Of course, few people attempt to go *only* by their feelings or to be *consistently* selfless—and the few who do don't live for long. Merely to keep breathing, a person must use logic and be selfish to some degree. Thus, people who accept the idea that being moral consists in being self*less* have to cheat on their moral convictions just to stay alive. While they sacrifice their own interests to some degree, as they believe morally, in order to be good, they should—they also pursue their own interests to some degree, as they know selfishly, in order to live, they must.

Aware that this means they are not being fully moral, such people rationalize their selfish pursuits with slogans such as "Nobody's perfect" and "Morality is not black and white." Simultaneously, they sabotage their personal interests with slogans such as "You have to compromise" and "Don't set your sights so high." This means they have accepted the notion that moral consistency is incompatible with personal happiness. Thus, they betray *both*—by instituting a personal policy of moral compromise. In so doing, they cut themselves off from life as it ought to be and settle for a semi-guilty, semi-repressed, watered-down sort of happiness.

If "morally" you *should* be selfless, but "practically" you *must* be selfish, then life is an obscene paradox: The moral and the practical are hopelessly at odds; being good is not good for you.

A solution to this dilemma requires the discovery of a morality that neither requires nor permits the sacrifice of anyone to anyone. What is needed is a *non-sacrificial* morality—a code of values that accounts for the actual, long-term, material and spiritual requirements of human life. But such a code, to be defended, must be based on a foundation other than faith or feelings, and such a foundation is thought to be impossible.

So the debate between religion and secular subjectivism continues, with both sides accepting the premise that an absolute morality requires the existence of God. The religionists fearfully assert: "God *must* exist. And since you can't prove that He doesn't, I say that He does and that His moral law is absolute. Being moral consists in glorifying God, obeying His commandments, and sacrificing in service of His higher purpose." To which the secular subjectivists skeptically reply: "You can't prove the existence of God, so I don't accept it. I say his so-called moral law is your Sunday-school fantasy. Morality is *not* absolute; it is a matter of personal preference or social convention. If I (or my group) say something, *that's* the moral law. And, yes, there will be sacrifices, but they will not be for your imaginary God; they will be for me (or my collective)."

Hence the alleged alternative: Either sacrifice yourself or sacrifice others. In other words, your choice is: masochism or sadism.

That is not a good alternative.

If we want to live happily—if we want to pursue our values guiltlessly, with integrity—we need a third alternative; we need to discover a *non-sacrificial* code of morality. And to defend such a code, we need to ground it logically in observable facts; we need to discover a natural, provable, *objective* standard of value on which to base it. Without such a code built on such a foundation, the sacrificial moralities of subjectivism are unanswerable. And on the terms of such moralities, a life of genuine happiness is unattainable.

Yes, there is a non-sacrificial code of morality—and an objective standard of value on which it is based. But on the road to their discovery, there appears to be an obstacle.

2

The Is–Ought Gap

Subjectivism's Technical Retreat

As we have seen, subjectivism—whether "supernatural," social, or personal—fails to provide proper guidance for human action, because each version calls for human sacrifice and leads to human suffering. If we want to live and achieve genuine happiness, we need a non-sacrificial alternative that is grounded in the facts of reality. But in search of such an alternative, we are faced with a big problem: The world is *full* of facts.

In fact, facts are all there are out there: Paris is a city in France. The Earth revolves around the Sun. Men are mortal. Acorns are potential oak trees. Computers are man-made objects. For every action, there is an equal and opposite reaction. Electrons surround the nucleus of an atom. Fire is hotter than ice. Some grass is green. People make choices. Mountains are bigger than molehills. A bush cannot speak. "Think" is a verb. The stock market rises and falls. The list goes on and on.

But where among all the facts is morality? Behind a tree? Up in the sky? On the Web? In a crystal? Where?

The problem is that in just looking around, facts appear to be everywhere, but morality does not appear to be anywhere. Our task is to discover moral principles in a world full of facts.

To begin, note that we can identify facts on several levels. Some are directly perceivable (fire is hotter than ice; some grass is green; the Sun rises). Others must be logically inferred (heat is a function of the motion of atoms; color is a function of the wave-lengths of light; the Earth revolves around the Sun). With our five senses, we can observe countless facts at the concrete, *perceptual* level. And with the power of our minds, we can infer even more facts on the abstract, *conceptual* level. The faculty that enables us to advance from the perceptual level (which we share with other animals) to the conceptual level (which is distinctive to human beings) is: reason.

Reason enables us to form concepts, to use language, to discover causal relationships, and to make the logical connections necessary for the achievement of our goals. It is our means of understanding the world in ever deeper and wider ways and of applying our discoveries to our chosen ends. But reason allows us to identify facts and *only* facts, which alone do not seem to tell us anything about what we morally ought to do. There simply is no *fact* labeled "ought" out there.

This is a serious problem. As human beings, we *need* moral guidance. Without moral guidance, how do we know the right way to spend our time or where best to put our effort? How do we know whether we should work for a living or steal from others or beg for handouts? How do we know whether we should tell the truth always or sometimes or never? How do we know if we should befriend someone, do business with him, trust him with our children, support his campaign, or grant him our vote? And how do we know the proper way to deal with criminals, tyrants, or terrorists?

In order to live and achieve happiness, we need to know how to evaluate our alternatives; we need to know how in principle we should act. In order to establish and maintain relationships conducive to our life and happiness, we need to know how in principle we should evaluate and respond to the actions of other people. And in order to define and defend the social conditions necessary for a life of happiness, we need to know what in essence they are.

So, since facts are all there are out there, and since reason is our means of discovering and understanding facts, the question we must answer is: How can we use reason to derive moral principles—principles regarding what people *ought* to do—from the facts of reality—from what *is?*

Now, at first blush an answer might seem pretty straightforward: Pick a goal, determine what you have to do in order to accomplish it—and there's your "ought." But not so fast. The *moral* question is: How does one choose a *proper* goal? If morality were a matter of picking and accomplishing any old goal, then a bank robber would be "moral" if he successfully robbed a bank; a swindler would be "moral" providing he never got caught; the Nazis, Communists, and priests of the Inquisition would have to be considered "moral" because they successfully tortured and slaughtered the people whom they chose to torture and slaughter; and the terrorists of Black Tuesday would have to be considered "moral" because they succeeded in *their* mission.

Logically, morality cannot be a matter of doing whatever one chooses to do; it cannot be a means of achieving arbitrary goals or ends. If moral ends were arbitrary, there would be no such thing as "good" and "evil"; there would be only "works" and "doesn't work." As in: If you want to have a lot of unearned money, robbing a bank works; robbing a parking meter doesn't. Or: If you want to suppress rational thought on a grand scale, theocracy works; mere scolding from the pulpit doesn't. Or: If you want to murder millions of innocent people, gas chambers, killing fields, and anthrax-loaded crop dusters work; a lone gunman doesn't. In other words, if moral ends are arbitrary, there is no such thing as morality—"anything goes."

If there *is* such a thing as morality, it is not merely an issue of effective means; it is also—and more fundamentally—a matter of proper ends. The concept of "morality" logically presupposes a proper end; without such an end, morality cannot exist. So the question is: What is a proper end?

An *end* is a goal toward which one acts; a *means* is the action one takes toward a goal. For instance, if a student studies in order to get an education, the education is an end toward which his studying is the means. Likewise, if a person works in order to earn a paycheck, the paycheck is an end toward which his work is the means. But notice that such goals are not ends in themselves. A student gets an education so that he can pursue a career—which he pursues in order to support himself and earn a paycheck— which he earns in order to buy things—which he buys in order to use for various other purposes—which he pursues in order to accomplish still other goals—and so on. Each end presupposes another. So where does it all end?

If we are to establish an objective, fact-based morality, we need to discover a *final* end—one toward which all of our other goals and values are properly aimed. Such an end is by that fact our standard of moral value—the standard against which we can objectively assess the value of all our choices and actions. So the question becomes: What is our *ultimate* goal?

Now, one would hope that we could turn to philosophers for some assistance here; after all, it is their job to answer such questions. But, alas, most philosophers hold that an ultimate goal or standard of moral value cannot be rationally justified. Philosophy professor Lionel Ruby explains the essence of this popular position as follows:

> [Goals] are like standards, in that some are more basic than others. Any goal short of the "ultimate" can be justified by a more basic goal. But a truly ultimate standard or goal cannot be justified by logic, for a proof requires a premise—in this case a value premise—and "ultimate" means "nothing more basic." . . . [Thus] truly ultimate standards or ends . . . are beyond the scope of logic and scientific evidence.[1]

This widespread belief underlies and gives rise to the problem known as the "is–ought" dichotomy, according to which it is impossible to move logically from the facts of reality—from what "is"—to moral principles—principles about how people "ought" to act. As Professor Ruby states the problem:

> Every value conclusion must rest on value premises. The "ought-to-be" can be deduced only from another "ought-to-be," and never from a mere "is" or statement of fact. A premise that merely states that something is or is not the case cannot yield a value conclusion.[2]

---

1. Lionel Ruby, *Logic: An Introduction* (Chicago: Lippincott, 1960), p. 498.
2. Ibid., p. 496.

This dual claim—that ultimate ends cannot be justified by logic and, thus, that moral principles cannot be grounded in facts—was first made in the eighteenth century by the Scottish philosopher David Hume (from whom we will hear shortly).[3] "The essence of Hume's view," explains Cambridge professor C. D. Broad, "is that Reason is wholly confined to matters of fact."

> It will help us to analyse a situation, to choose means for a given end, and to infer probable consequences of various alternative courses of action. But it has nothing whatever to do with our choice of ends as distinct from means. We desire things as ends only because they move some emotion in us, and not because of any objective characteristic in them which Reason can recognise.[4]

Not surprisingly, this notion breeds moral subjectivism. And unfortunately, it is almost universally accepted among intellectuals today.

Princeton professor Peter Singer declares that "The gap between facts and values remains as unbridgeable as it was when David Hume first drew attention to it in 1739. . . ."[5] UCLA professor James Q. Wilson tells us: "I learned from Hume, as did legions of my fellow students, that this transition is impossible; one cannot infer an 'ought' statement from an 'is' statement; in modern parlance, one cannot infer values from facts. It is logically untenable."[6] And in a textbook titled *Attacking Faulty Reasoning,* Professor T. Edward Damer writes: "It is not logically sound to move in an argument from a factual claim, a so-called 'is,' to a

---

3. See David Hume, *Enquiries Concerning Human Understanding and Concerning the Principles of Morals* (Oxford: Clarendon Press, 1975), Appendix I, esp. pp. 287–89, 292–94; and *Treatise of Human Nature* (Oxford: Clarendon Press, 1978), Book III, esp. pp. 457–59, 462–70.
4. C.D. Broad, *Five Types of Ethical Theory* (New York: Harcourt, Brace & Company, 1934), p. 107. Cf. Bertrand Russell, *Human Society in Ethics and Politics* (New York: Simon and Schuster, 1955), pp. vi–vii.
5. Peter Singer, *A Darwinian Left* (New Haven: Yale University Press, 1999), p. 12.
6. James Q. Wilson, *The Moral Sense* (New York: Free Press Paperbacks, 1993), p. 237.

moral claim, a so-called 'ought.' To do so is to commit the well-known 'is–ought' fallacy."[7]

On this view, to recognize the facts of a given situation, and to try to use those facts in order to discover and take a moral course of action, is to commit a "logical fallacy." Apparently, to be moral, one should disregard everything one knows to be true and act solely according to one's unfettered desires or the norms of one's tribe. Some advice.

The is–ought problem may seem silly, but if left unsolved it has serious consequences. If facts have no bearing on what a person morally ought to do—if reason is merely a means of achieving subjectively chosen ends—if morality cannot be grounded objectively in reality—if there is an unbridgeable gap between "is" and "ought," between facts and values—then, as Professor Ruby notes, we have only "personal preference or the approval of our group as the ultimate basis for our value-judgments."[8] And we know what that means.

The is–ought gap is the secular subjectivists' technical retreat. It serves as their linguistic asylum from the imposition of any moral standards. It is their ticket to "get away" with whatever they (or their group) *feel* like doing. And it is why no one can answer them when they say: "There are no moral absolutes" or "Morality is not black and white" or "Who's to say what's right?"

People who make such claims are counting on our inability to name a fact-based, logically provable, *objective* standard of moral value. Consciously or not, they are relying on the is–ought dichotomy to defend moral subjectivism. And, consciously or not, they are supported by the likes of David Hume and the legions of subjectivist college professors who each year teach another batch of future intellectuals that moral principles cannot be derived from the facts of reality.

What do Hume and company propose as an alternative? How, in their view, are people supposed to determine what is morally right and wrong? How are we to distinguish virtue from vice?

---

7. T. Edward Damer, *Attacking Faulty Reasoning*, 3rd ed. (Belmont: Wadsworth, 1995), p. 10.
8. Ruby, *Logic: An Introduction*, p. 498.

Their answer: By reference to a "moral sense," which they also call "sentiments of pleasure and uneasiness" and, you guessed it: "feelings."

According to Hume, if you see a man raping a woman, you cannot say that what you are witnessing is *factually* immoral; you cannot say that as a matter of fact he should not be doing that. No matter how you view the situation, all you can say in terms of facts is: There is a woman kicking and screaming furiously while a man is eagerly trying to have sex with her; the man has made a choice, and the woman appears to think differently about it. As to a moral judgment—as to whether the man is being virtuous or vicious—that, says Hume, depends solely on how it makes you *feel* inside.

Lest it seem that I am exaggerating Hume's position, here it is in his own words: "An action, or sentiment, or character is virtuous or vicious; why? Because its view causes a pleasure or uneasiness of a particular kind."

> Take any action allowed to be vicious: Wilful murder, for instance. Examine it in all lights, and see if you can find that matter of fact, or real existence, which you call *vice*. In whichever way you take it, you find only certain passions, motives, volitions and thoughts. There is no other matter of fact in the case. The vice entirely escapes you, as long as you consider the object [the observable facts]. You never can find it, till you turn your reflexion into your own breast, and find a sentiment of disapprobation [moral disapproval], which arises in you, towards this action.[9]

Disturbed by that, you might demand a firm answer: Tell me, Mr. Hume, is it your position that rapists and murderers are vicious or not! His answer: "When you pronounce any action or character to be vicious, you mean nothing, but that from the constitution of your nature you have a feeling or a sentiment of blame from the contemplation of it."[10] In other words, to condemn

---

9. Hume, *Treatise of Human Nature*, Book III, pp. 468–69, spelling modernized.
10. Ibid., p. 469.

murderers and rapists as immoral is merely to express your emotional discomfort at the thought of what they do.[11]

If moral judgments cannot be grounded in the facts of reality,
then we are in a moral vacuum; logic is merely a means to achieving arbitrarily chosen ends; swindlers, hoodlums, Nazis, communists,
terrorists, and religious "inquisitors" are neither moral nor immoral—
only successful or unsuccessful. If so, human sacrifices of any kind
and degree can be "justified" by the decree of any common crimi-
nal, any collective, any dictator, any "prophet," or any pope.

The problem is not: "If there is no God, anything goes." The
problem is: If there is no objective standard of value, anything
goes. If there is no rationally provable standard of value, there is
no way to defend with moral certainty what is right or to condemn with moral certainty what is wrong. The alternative is not
religion versus subjectivism, but *reason* versus subjectivism—and
the secular subjectivists know it.

Hitler did not fear religion or faith; he feared reason and logic.
He saw the Church not as an enemy but as a *mentor,* because of
its remarkable ability to get people to believe in a creed full of
contradictions. Here, in his own words, is Hitler acknowledging
his heartfelt debt to religion:

> The Church has never allowed the Creed to be interfered with.
> It is fifteen hundred years since it was formulated, but every
> suggestion for its amendment, every logical criticism or attack
> on it, has been rejected. The Church has realized that anything
> and everything can be built up on a document of that sort, no
> matter how contradictory or irreconcilable with it. The faithful
> will swallow it whole, so long as logical reasoning is never al-
> lowed to be brought to bear on it.[12]

Hitler's plans *required* that people have faith; thus, he had
nothing but contempt for logic. And he was neither the first nor
the last to feel this way. David Hume was as explicit about his hatred of reason as he was about his love for feelings. Just as he in-

---

11. Cf. Gilbert Harman, *The Nature of Morality* (New York: Oxford University
    Press, 1977), esp. pp. 11, 27–28, 32–33.
12. Adolf Hitler, quoted in Hermann Rauschning, *The Voice of Destruction* (New
    York: Putnam, 1940), pp. 239–40.

sisted that feelings are our only moral guides, so he insisted that "Reason is, and ought only to be the slave of the passions, and can never pretend to any other office than to serve and obey them." What does that mean? Hume tells us: "It is not contrary to reason to prefer the destruction of the whole world to the scratching of my finger."[13]

Now, we know what Hitler's hatred of reason led to, but what about Hume's? After all, he was not a maniacal mass murderer, but a peaceful philosopher who merely taught legions of other philosophers that moral principles cannot be derived from the facts of reality. What harm could that do?

Well, ideas have consequences. And Hume's ideas have made their way from the minds of ivory-tower philosophers into the minds of regular people. They have even made their way into the minds of children. Recall who said this: "My belief is that if I say something, it goes. I am the law, and if you don't like it, you die. If I don't like you or I don't like what you want me to do, you die." It was Eric Harris of the Columbine massacre. Is it any wonder what ideas got into his head? How far is his philosophy from this one: "It is not contrary to reason to prefer the destruction of the whole world to the scratching of my finger"?

Subjectivism—whether personal, social, or "supernatural"—wreaks havoc on human life and happiness. Until we can answer it with (genuine) moral certainty—that is, until we can *show* that morality is based on facts—it will continue to do so. From muggings and rapes, to school shootings and truck bombings, to concentration camps and gulags, to religious "inquisitions" and divinely inspired acts of terrorism—all such mayhem is caused by subjectivism. And the is–ought dichotomy is what makes subjectivism seem plausible.

The is–ought gap represents a moral abyss. If we care about human life and happiness, we need to bridge it. We need to ground morality in reality; we need to discover a rationally provable ultimate end—a standard of value derived from observation and logic.

Fortunately, the problem has been solved; the gap has been bridged; morality has been tied to reality. An objective standard of value has been rationally proved, and it is the subject of our next chapter.

---

13. Hume, *Treatise of Human Nature,* Book II, pp. 415–16, spelling modernized.

3

To Be Or Not To Be

The Basic Choice

In Chapter 2, we encountered the problem known as the "is–ought" dichotomy, the notion that moral principles (principles regarding what people "ought" to do) cannot be derived from the facts of reality (from what "is"). We also saw that this problem persists for lack of an observation-based, objective standard of value. Here we turn to the solution to that problem. First, we will discover just such a standard; then, we will discover a number of objective moral principles—principles in accordance with that standard.

To begin, note that the basic fact that makes morality such a difficult subject is the very fact that makes it a subject in the first place: free will. As human beings we have the faculty of volition, the power of choice; we choose our actions. This fact gives rise to our need of morality. Indeed, the realm of morality *is* the realm of choice. What makes the issue complicated is the fact that our choices are guided by our values—*which are also chosen*. This is why it is so difficult to get to the bottom of morality: Human values are chosen—*every last one of them*. Consequently, peoples' values seem to differ in every imaginable way.

Some people choose to play soccer; they value footwork, teamwork, and winning. Some choose to dance ballet; they value grace, poise, and flight. And some choose to attend church; they value sermons, faith, and prayer. A person who goes hiking values the scenery and exercise. One who goes fishing values the nibble

and catch. And one who takes heroin values the so-called "high."
A person who steals jewelry values "free stuff." One who makes
jewelry values craftsmanship. A sculptor values the process of creating art. A software developer values *that* creative process. A student who cheats on a test values "getting away" with it. One who
studies for the test values the knowledge he gains thereby. A doctor specializing in internal medicine values the process of curing
disease. A terrorist specializing in biological warfare values the
process of spreading disease. A man who treats his wife with respect values certain qualities in her. One who abuses his wife values having power over her. A General who fights for mandatory
"volunteerism" values involuntary servitude. One who fights to
defend individual rights values freedom. And so on. Different people act in different ways; they value different things.

So the question is: How do we know if our choice of values
is good or bad, right or wrong? What is our *standard* of value?

As we have already seen, if we do not consciously hold *something* as our standard of value, then we have nothing by reference
to which we can determine what goals we should or should not
pursue—how we should or should not act. And if we do not hold
something *rationally provable* as our standard of value, then we
default to some form of subjectivism—personal, social, or "supernatural"—which can lead only to human sacrifice, suffering, and
death. If we want to live and achieve happiness, we need a non-
sacrificial standard of value that is grounded in perceptual evidence—facts we can see.

In search of such a standard, the proper approach is to turn
not to personal opinion or social convention or "super-nature," but
to *actual nature* and ask, as the American philosopher Ayn Rand
did: "What are *values?* Why does man need them?"

Generally speaking, a person's values are the things he cares
about, the things he is interested in, the things he pursues or protects. A "value," observes Ayn Rand, is "that which one acts to
gain and/or keep."[1] The key word here is: acts. Plants, animals,
and people act; rocks, rivers, and hammers do not. Trees, for ex-

---

1. Ayn Rand, "The Objectivist Ethics," in *The Virtue of Selfishness* (New York:
   Signet, 1964), p. 16.

ample, extend their roots into the ground and their branches and leaves toward the sky; they value minerals, water, and sunlight. Snakes hunt, strike, and struggle to keep the critters they catch; they value crickets, frogs, and mice. Rabbits nibble on plants and hide in hollows; they value vegetation and shelter. People grow crops, build houses, make friends, and go to school; we value nutrition, shelter, other people, and education. *All living organisms take self-generated, goal-directed action.*[2]

Non-living things, on the other hand, take no such action. They can be moved, but they cannot act—not in the self-generated, goal-directed sense that living things do. A rock just remains wherever it is unless some outside force, such as a wave or a hammer, hits and moves it. A river flows, but its motion is not self-generated; water moves only by means of some outside force—in this case, the gravitational pull of the earth. And a hammer does not, by itself, smash rocks or drive nails; it does not generate its own action.

The reason why inanimate objects do not act in the same sense that living things do is that they have no needs and therefore no corresponding means of action. Rocks, rivers, and hammers do not need or value anything; thus, they have no means of gaining or keeping anything. Only living organisms have needs, values, or goals; accordingly, only they have a means of acting toward such ends.

"The concept 'value' is not a primary," continues Ayn Rand; "it presupposes an answer to the question: of value to *whom* and for *what?* It presupposes an entity capable of acting to achieve a goal in the face of an alternative."[3] A tree faces the alternative of reaching water and sunlight—or not; a snake faces the alternative of catching and keeping its prey—or not; a rabbit faces the alternative of finding food and shelter—or not; and a person faces the alternative of achieving his goals—or not.

The objects that a living thing acts to gain or keep are *its* values—values *to* it. That answers the question: "to *whom?*" But the question: "for *what?*" remains.

---

2. See Rand, *For the New Intellectual,* p. 121; and "The Objectivist Ethics," pp. 16–17.
3. Rand, "The Objectivist Ethics," p. 16.

What difference does it make whether or not an organism achieves its goals? What happens if it succeeds, and what happens if it fails? What *ultimately* is at stake? Here is Ayn Rand's key passage on the issue:

> There is only one fundamental alternative in the universe: existence or non-existence—and it pertains to a single class of entities: to living organisms. The existence of inanimate matter is unconditional, the existence of life is not: it depends on a specific course of action. Matter is indestructible, it changes forms, but it cannot cease to exist. It is only a living organism that faces a constant alternative: the issue of life or death. Life is a process of self-sustaining and self-generated action. If an organism fails in that action, it dies; its chemical elements remain, but its life goes out of existence. It is only the concept of "Life" that makes the concept of "Value" possible.[4]

The reason why living things need values is: in order to *live*. The answer to the question "for *what?*" is: for *life*.

For hundreds of years philosophers have been stumped by the problem of how to derive moral principles, principles regarding what people *ought* to do, from the facts of reality, from what *is*. By showing that values are certain kinds of facts—facts in relation to the requirements of life—Ayn Rand has solved the problem.

> In answer to those philosophers who claim that no relation can be established between ultimate ends or values and the facts of reality, let me stress that the fact that living entities exist and function necessitates the existence of values and of an ultimate value which for any given living entity is its own life. Thus the validation of value judgments is to be achieved by reference to the facts of reality. The fact that a living entity *is*, determines what it *ought* to do.[5]

A living thing's *life* is its ultimate goal; its life is the final end toward which its actions are the means; its life is its ultimate

4. Ibid.
5. Ibid., p. 18.

value. Ayn Rand's crucial discovery here is the fact that *life is the standard of value.* And human beings are no exception to this principle. People need values for the same reason plants and animals do: in order to sustain and further their life. A person's life is his ultimate value. *Man's* life is the standard of *moral* value.[6]

Now, it is true that in the absence of an ultimate goal it would be impossible to derive moral principles from the facts of reality. But there is no such situation for man—and there never could be. A person does not and cannot live without an ultimate goal, because his choice to remain alive establishes his life as his ultimate goal. If he chooses to continue living, reality (what *is*) dictates what he *ought* to do: He ought to pursue the values necessary to sustain and further his life. If he chooses *not* to continue living, he has no need of values: He can simply stop acting altogether, and he will soon die.

But, one might ask, doesn't free will make the issue subjective? Can't a person choose a different standard of value if he wants to?

No, free will does not make the issue subjective. It *does* mean that a person can choose not to live; but it does *not* mean that he can choose a standard of value other than life.

As Ayn Rand pointed out, the alternative of existence or nonexistence is the only *fundamental* alternative; all other alternatives are derivatives of it. Consider, for instance, the following: food or poison, pleasure or pain, knowledge or ignorance, joy or sorrow, creation or destruction, wealth or poverty, trade or theft, freedom or slavery. What makes these alternatives possible? *Life* makes them possible. Without life they would not and could not exist. Without life there would be no one to whom anything could be beneficial or harmful. And why do such alternatives matter one way or the other? Because of the requirements of *life*. They are values or non-values only in relation to the alternative of life or death—and only for the purpose of promoting one's life. The fact that we have free will does not change any of this; it simply grants us a choice in the matter: to live or not to live—to be or not to be.

---

6. See Rand, "The Objectivist Ethics," pp. 17, 27; and *For the New Intellectual*, pp. 121–22.

The choice *to be* underlies and makes possible all of our other choices—and thus all of our other values. We cannot make any choice or value anything apart from the choice to continue living. The choice to do homework presupposes it; the choice to build a business presupposes it; the choice to compose a symphony presupposes it; the choice to go surfing presupposes it; the choice to make love presupposes it; and so on. All such choices depend on the choice to live. But the choice to live does not presuppose any other choice; it is the one choice on which all other choices depend. It is the most basic choice of all.

Moreover, just as our choice to remain alive makes our pursuit of values *possible,* so it makes our pursuit of values *necessary.* To continue living, we must act to gain the values on which our life depends, such as knowledge, food, shelter, and medical care. So the point is not merely that we have to *be* alive in order to pursue values, but also that we have to pursue values in order to *stay* alive—and, further (since we have free will), that we must pursue values by *choice.*[7] Put negatively: Just as we cannot pursue values unless we choose to continue living, so we cannot continue living unless we choose to pursue values.

In sum, there is no ultimate goal or value other than life *to which* a person can pledge his allegiance, because there is no fundamental alternative other than existence or non-existence *with which* a person is faced. Life or death is it: A person either strives for self-preservation or courts self-elimination. In order to live, he has to pursue values; in order to die, he does not.

In a nutshell, Ayn Rand's key ethical discovery is the fact that the concept of "value" presupposes, depends on, and derives from the concept of "life." And since the choice to remain alive (or not) is the only fundamental choice, human life is logically the standard of moral value—and the only possible one.

Now, because people have free will, a person *can* choose to remain alive and then take anti-life actions. In fact, altruism encourages people to do just that: to sacrifice their life-serving values for the sake of God or other people. But a person cannot do so *consistently;* he cannot act against his life (his ultimate value)

---

7. Cf. Leonard Peikoff, *Objectivism: The Philosophy of Ayn Rand* (New York: Meridian, 1993), pp. 213–14.

as a matter of unwavering principle, or he will quickly die. (This is why, as we saw in Chapter 1, altruists have to cheat on their morality just to stay alive.) The only values a person can pursue consistently are those that are conducive to his survival and happiness. The only values he can seek as a matter of unwavering principle are those that promote his life.

Morality *is* chosen—all the way down to one's standard of value. A person's choice to remain alive makes his life his ultimate value and thus gives rise to his need of morality. If he chooses *not* to live, he has no need of morality. And if he chooses to remain alive and then hypocritically acts *against* his life, that, too, is his choice—and the consequences are his to suffer. But if a person wants to stay alive and achieve happiness, he has to act in a manner that *promotes* his life and well-being. None other will do.

Moral principles are guides to human action for the purpose of sustaining and furthering one's life. And, not surprisingly, if a person chooses *consistently* to act in a life-promoting manner, then (disasters aside) he will achieve the kind of happiness that is consonant with the requirements of human life: *genuine* happiness. In other words, being good—acting in a life-promoting manner—*is* good for you; it furthers your life and results in true happiness.

If one *wants* to live happily, one *has* to act morally; one has to be loyal in action to one's ultimate value: one's life.

Ayn Rand's breakthrough is truly profound: It not only bridges the is–ought gap; it also solves the problem of human sacrifice. Given that life is the standard of value, what is the moral status of self-sacrifice? Does a person have a moral "duty" to sacrifice himself for the sake of others, God, or society? And what is the moral status of sacrificing other people? Does a person have a moral "right" to sacrifice others for his own sake? The answers are becoming clear.

Since each person is obviously a separate being with his own body, his own mind, his own life—since life is an attribute of the individual—each person's *own* life is his *own* ultimate value. Each individual is morally an end in himself—not a means to the ends of others.[8] Accordingly, a person has neither a moral duty to

---

8. See Ayn Rand, "Introducing Objectivism," in *The Voice of Reason* (New York: Meridian, 1990), p. 4.

sacrifice himself for the sake of others (as religion and social subjectivism claim) nor a moral right to sacrifice others for his own
sake (as personal subjectivism claims). On principle, neither self-
sacrifice nor sacrifice of others is moral, because, on principle,
human sacrifice *as such* is immoral.

Human life does not require people to sacrifice themselves
for the sake of others; nor does it require people to sacrifice
others for their own sake. Human life simply does not require human sacrifice; people *can* live without killing, beating, robbing,
or defrauding one another. Moreover, human sacrifice cannot
promote human life and happiness; it can lead only to suffering
and death. If people want to live and be happy, they must neither
sacrifice themselves nor sacrifice others; rather, they must pursue
life-serving values and respect the rights of others to do the same.

The moral principle here is: egoism.

Egoism holds that each individual ought to act in his own
best interest and is the proper beneficiary of his own moral action.[9] (*Ego* is Latin for *I* or *self;* "egoism" means "self-ism.") The
validity of egoism is implicit in the very *nature* of values. A
value is the object of an action taken by a living organism to sustain and further *its* life. Since human beings have free will, a person can choose to live or not to live. If he chooses to live, then
his life *is* his ultimate value, and he *ought* to be loyal in action
to that fact—he ought to take the actions necessary to sustain and
further his life. Such actions are, by definition, moral actions.
Conversely, if a person chooses to remain alive and then to betray his ultimate value—to act against his life—he is, by definition, acting immorally.

It is crucial here to clearly distinguish egoism from hedonism
and personal subjectivism. True egoism—rational egoism—does
not hold "pleasure" or "feelings" as the standard of value. It holds
life as the standard of value—and happiness as the moral purpose
of life.[10] Many actions that might "please" a person or make him
"feel" good for the moment *do not* actually promote his life, and

---

9. See Peikoff, *Objectivism,* pp. 229–30.
10. See Rand, "The Objectivist Ethics," pp. 32–33.

thus *are not* actually in his best interest. For instance, a salesman might *feel* like snoozing the alarm one morning, but if it means missing an important meeting or losing a key customer, then it is not in his best interest. Likewise, a ballerina might get *pleasure* from eating lots of cake and ice cream, but if it means putting on weight that will ruin her career, then it is not good for her life. And a married man might *feel* like sleeping with another woman, but if it is going to destroy his integrity, his self-respect, and his marriage, then it is not going to make him happy. A person who allows himself to be guided by his feelings is *not* being selfish. He is being *un*selfish.

Every thinking adult knows that the mere fact that one *wants* to do something does not necessarily mean it is in one's best interest to do it. This is why neither hedonism nor personal subjectivism is egoistic: Both advocate action guided by sheer desire—a policy that, far from advancing one's life, is guaranteed to destroy it. If one wants to live and achieve happiness, one has to be *genuinely* egoistic; one has to act in a *life-promoting* manner.

The next question is: How do we know what constitutes life-promoting action? The principle of egoism says that we *should* act to further our life, but it does not give us any specific guidance as to what goals or actions will serve that purpose. To answer this question, we must again turn to (actual) nature and observe the relevant facts. And in so doing, we must bear in mind the following.

We are not simple creatures; we are complex beings of body and mind—matter and spirit—whose values pertain to both aspects of this integrated whole. Nor do we live for just a moment or a day; human life is an ongoing process spanning years and decades. Thus, living properly (being moral) consists in pursuing life-serving values not sporadically or occasionally, but regularly and consistently—as a matter of principle.

In order to do so, we need both long-range and wide-range guidance: long-range guidance to account for the span of our lifetime, and wide-range guidance to account for the broad spectrum of our needs. To determine whether an action is good or bad, helpful or harmful to our life, we have to project both the physical and the psychological consequences—and not only with regard to the present, but also with regard to the more distant future. Our means of doing so are moral principles—principles grounded in the dual fact that human life is the standard of moral value and personal happiness is the moral purpose of one's life. Such principles are the subject of the remainder of the book.

4

Objective Moral Values

Basic Human Needs

We have seen that human life is logically the standard of moral value—and that each individual's own life is logically his own ultimate value. Here we turn to the question of the human means of survival. What *things* do we need in order to live? What *actions* must we take in order to gain and keep those things? And, most importantly: What makes those actions *possible?*

All living things have a means of survival. Plants survive by means of their automatic *vegetative* process known as photosynthesis. Animals survive by means of their automatic *instinctive* processes such as hunting, fleeing, and nest building. Human beings, however, do not survive by automatic means; our means of survival is not instinctual, but *volitional.* Since we have free will, we choose to live or not to live—and if we choose to live, we must also choose to discover the requirements of our life and to act accordingly.

While the choice to live is up to us, the basic requirements of our life are determined by nature. In order to live, we must take a specific course of action; random action will not do. We cannot survive by eating rocks, drinking Drano, or wandering aimlessly in the desert; and we cannot achieve happiness through procrastination, promiscuity, or pot. If we want to live and enjoy life, we have to discover and act in accordance with the actual, *objective* requirements of our survival and happiness. What are they?

To zero in on the most basic of these requirements, suppose you were alone on an island. What would you have to do in order to survive? At a bare minimum you would need food, clothing, and shelter; so we can begin by considering what you would have to do to get them. In order to obtain food, you would have to hunt and fish, gather nuts and berries, plant and harvest crops, build and control fires, and prepare and cook meals. In order to acquire clothing, you would have to skin animals, clean and tan their hides, measure yourself for size, lay out a pattern, cut it to shape, and stitch it together. In order to procure shelter, you would have to establish a suitable location, gather appropriate materials, and build a structure capable of shielding yourself from the elements and from any animals that might want to eat you. In order to accomplish these goals, you would have to fashion the necessary tools such as clubs, spears, bows, and arrows; hooks, lines, and sinkers; knives and cookware; needles and thread; measuring devices, props and fasteners. And each of these objectives would require a number of subordinate tasks such as whittling, twisting, braiding, pounding, chopping, aligning, lashing, and so forth.

In short, you would have to take materials from the environment and transform them into your means of survival. You would have to reshape the available resources and create the values on which your life depends. In a word, you would have to be *productive*.

Of course, in a specialized society we can buy food from a supermarket, clothing from a department store, and a home from a realtor. But our ability to purchase such goods presupposes both that someone has produced them and that we have produced something to trade in exchange for them. So the fact remains: Whether alone on an island or among others in a society, if one wants to live, one has to be productive.

And human life requires much more than just food, clothing, and shelter; it requires a multitude of values. Consider the vast number of things that support and enhance our life: furniture, electricity, machinery, medicine, books, airplanes, plumbing, computers, automobiles, schools, cinemas, sports facilities, works of art, libraries, and so forth. All such things come from people being productive.

Productive work is essential to human life; it makes human life possible.

What happens if a person refuses to be productive? If he is alone on an island, he dies. And if a person refuses to be productive while he is among others in a society, he becomes a parasite on those who do choose to be productive; he becomes a pauper, a beggar, or a thief. In order to live *as a human being* (rather than as a parasite), a person *has to be productive.*

It is clear that human life depends on productive work. Our next question is: What does productive work depend on? What is it that enables us to transform raw materials into human values? It is our ability to *think*—to observe facts, to form concepts, to discover causal relationships, and to use logic. While other animals acquire their values by means of instinct, we have to engage in a process of thought. As Ayn Rand put it:

> Man cannot survive, as animals do, by the guidance of mere percepts. A sensation of hunger will tell him that he needs food (if he has learned to identify it as "hunger"), but it will not tell him how to obtain his food and it will not tell him what food is good for him or poisonous. He cannot provide for his simplest physical needs without a process of thought. He needs a process of thought to discover how to plant and grow his food or how to make weapons for hunting. His percepts might lead him to a cave, if one is available—but to build the simplest shelter, he needs a process of thought. No percepts and no "instincts" will tell him how to light a fire, how to weave cloth, how to forge tools, how to make a wheel, how to make an airplane, how to perform an appendectomy, how to produce an electric light bulb or an electronic tube or a cyclotron or a box of matches. Yet his life depends on such knowledge—and only a volitional act of his consciousness, a process of thought, can provide it.[1]

In order to live we have to be productive; in order to be productive we have to *think;* and the faculty that makes thinking possible is *reason.* While other animals survive by means of instinct,

---

1. Rand, "The Objectivist Ethics," pp. 22–23.

we have to use reason—and we have to do so by *choice.* Quoting Ayn Rand again:

> Reason does not work automatically; thinking is not a mechanical process; the connections of logic are not made by instinct. The function of your stomach, lungs or heart is automatic; the function of your mind is not. In any hour and issue of your life, you are free to think or to evade that effort. But you are not free to escape from your nature, from the fact that *reason* is your means of survival—so that for *you,* who are a human being, the question "to be or not to be" is the question "to think or not to think."[2]

Human life depends on productive work, and productive work depends on reason. Productivity is a process of value creation governed entirely by the rational functions of the human mind. If a person moves materials around without thinking, he will not create values; he will only make a mess (for examples see Marxist politics and modern art). Human values can come into existence only by means of productive effort guided by rational thinking.

Rational thinking is the most basic requirement of human life; it is the process on which human life most fundamentally depends.

What happens if a person refuses to think? If he is alone on an island, he dies. Even wild berries have to be identified as edible before they can be used to support human life; identifying them as edible requires a process of rational thought. And what happens if a person refuses to think while he is among others in a society? He becomes a parasite on those who do choose to think. In order to live *as a human being,* a person *has to use reason.*

The purpose of thinking is to understand the world and our needs so that we can pursue our values and live. Since life is the standard of value, and since reason is our most basic means of living, it follows that reason is our most basic value.

Being *moral* is a matter of being *rational*—which means: looking at the facts of reality, discovering the requirements of our life and long-term happiness, producing the values that support and

---

2. Rand, *For the New Intellectual,* p. 120.

enhance our life, and enjoying the process of living as a human being.

Let us now turn our attention to this last issue: enjoying life.

The fact that we must think in order to live is a relatively straightforward matter. The more difficult but equally important question concerns the role of our feelings. If reason is our guide to living and enjoying life, where do our emotions fit into the picture?

To answer this question, we need to discover the nature and source of our emotions—what they are and how they come to be. In so doing, we will see that emotions are as necessary to our life as reason is—but that they serve a very different role, which, if we are to achieve and maintain happiness, must be recognized and respected.

In order to live, we have to acquire knowledge, form convictions, and make value judgments—judgments regarding what is good or bad, for or against our life. These three things—our knowledge, our convictions (or beliefs), and our value judgments—are the spiritual *cause* of our emotions.

For example, if a hiker knows what rattlesnakes look like and judges them to be dangerous, then when he encounters one on the trail, he will feel some degree of fear. But if he does not know anything about them, or is unaware of their deadly nature, he might feel curious and try to pick it up. Similarly, if a hiker gets lost in the wilderness and runs out of food, he will feel relieved to discover a patch of wild berries—providing he believes them to be edible. If he thinks they might be poisonous, he will feel apprehensive about eating them.

Emotions are automatic responses arising from one's *ideas*— one's knowledge, beliefs, and value judgments—in relation to one's experiences.[3]

To further illustrate this point, consider three women who experience the same physical phenomenon, morning sickness, but have entirely different emotional reactions to it. The first woman wakes up feeling physically ill but becomes spiritually excited. She has been trying to get pregnant for over a year and knows that

---

3. See Peikoff, *Objectivism,* pp. 153–58.

this could be a good sign. The second woman has been trying to get pregnant, too, but when she wakes up feeling sick she becomes frustrated. She does not know the meaning of morning sickness and thinks she has the flu. The third woman wakes up feeling sick and panics. She knows all about morning sickness but had no intention of getting pregnant—and her religion forbids abortion.

While each woman has the same physical experience (morning sickness), each has a different emotional reaction to it. Why? Because each has a different set of ideas—knowledge, beliefs, and value judgments—in relation to which the experience is processed. Emotions are consequences of ideas.

Take another example. Three men hear the following news: "A chemical extract from the Pacific yew tree appears to be a promising new drug in the battle against cancer." When the first man hears this, he becomes irate. He believes that trees have a "right" to live and should not be cut down to save human lives. He believes that nature has "intrinsic" value—value "in and of itself," apart from any human purpose; thus, he believes that people have no right to use or exploit it for their selfish human ends. Further, since cancer is a part of nature too, he believes that it should be left alone to take its natural course. Consequently, this news about people tampering with nature to fight cancer just enrages him. The second man has a different reaction. When he hears about the drug, he feels a burst of hope. His wife has cancer, and since this man knows that the concept of "value" presupposes the question "of value to *whom* and for *what?*" he believes that nature has value only insofar as it can be used to serve human life—for instance, the life of his beloved. The third man experiences yet another reaction. When he hears the news, he feels a tinge of discomfort. He knows that such issues are controversial and believes that it is best to avoid the subject, to stay clear of the debate, and not to have any strong "opinions" about human life, nature, or cancer.

Again, while each man has the same experience (hears the same news), each has a different emotional reaction to it because each has accepted a different set of ideas.

Different ideas cause different emotions.

Our emotions are automatic results of our ideas (in relation to our experiences). As such, they are the psychological means by which we experience our values. When we receive good news or gain a value or accomplish a goal, we experience some kind and degree of psychological pleasure or joy—the basic *positive* emotion. When we receive bad news or lose a value or fail to accomplish a goal, we experience some kind and degree of psychological pain or suffering—the basic *negative* emotion.

For example, when a hard-working artist completes a beautiful sculpture, he experiences positive emotions such as elation and exaltation. Since he considers the event to be a good thing, he experiences psychological pleasure or joy. If he later discovers that an envious vandal has smashed the sculpture, he experiences negative emotions such as anger and grief. Since he considers *this* event to be a bad thing, he experiences psychological pain or suffering.

Observe further that if the artist's emotional reactions were reversed—if upon completing the sculpture he plunged into depression, and upon discovering it smashed he jumped for joy—this would mean that he has serious psychological problems.

Our emotional faculty serves as a gauge of our spiritual health. To the degree that our emotions are in harmony with the facts of reality, we are in good spiritual health. To the extent that our emotions are in conflict with the facts of reality, we have some spiritual work to do in this area. Such work can be difficult and time-consuming, but if a life of happiness is our goal, it is work we must do. And in order to do it, we need to know how.

The key to achieving and maintaining spiritual health lies in understanding the source of our ideas. We have seen that our emotions are consequences (effects) of our ideas (which are their cause). Our ideas, in turn, are consequences of our *thinking*—which can be rational or irrational, evidence-based or evidence-free, connected to reality or disconnected from it. If we want to achieve and maintain spiritual harmony, we must think rationally; we must accept only evidence-based ideas—ideas *connected* to reality. Such ideas give rise to healthy emotions—emotions in *harmony* with the facts. Conversely, we must not think irrationally; we must reject all evidence-free ideas—ideas *disconnected* from reality. Such ideas give rise to unhealthy emotions—emotions in *conflict* with the facts.

To illustrate this point, consider a person whose thinking *is* connected to reality and thus has led him to believe that trade is good and theft is bad. When he goes to the movies he will gladly pay the admission fee and will have no desire to sneak into the theater. His feelings about the financial transaction will be in harmony with reality—with the fact that human values (such as movies) are products of people's efforts and are made available to others only on the condition of trade.

Now, compare him to a person whose thinking is disconnected from reality and thus has led him to believe that trade is a nuisance and theft is the way to go. When he goes to the movies he will resent having to pay and will feel an urge to sneak in. His feelings about the transaction will be in conflict with reality. The solution to this emotional conflict is for the person to start thinking *rationally*. If he does, then, over time, his emotions will come into harmony with reality, and he will begin to feel like doing what is right instead of what is wrong. If he does not start thinking rationally, then his feelings will remain in conflict with the facts, and he will continue to feel like doing what is wrong instead of what is right.

Like the basic material requirements of human survival, the basic spiritual requirements of emotional harmony are determined not by us, but by nature. Just as we cannot survive by eating poisonous berries, playing in traffic, or leaving nature alone, so we cannot achieve happiness by robbing banks, sneaking into theaters, or lying our way into a job or a relationship. If we want our emotions to be in harmony with reality, we have to discover and uphold the actual requirements of that spiritual state.

The human mind is a specific kind of thing (a consciousness with free will) whose emotional harmony requires a specific kind of action (the commitment to keep its ideas connected to reality and to direct its body to act accordingly). If we want to achieve and maintain happiness, we have to think and act rationally.

As a final example, consider a child who is raised by racist parents and adopts their irrational ideas. Until and unless he decides to look at the evidence, think for himself, and replace the false ideas with true ones, he will experience unhealthy, harmful emotions. If he never embraces the responsibility of independent thinking, he will be plagued for life by twisted ideas, false value judgments, and their consequent emotions—which will sabotage his happiness. If, however, he does decide to think for himself, he will discover that his first-hand knowledge of the fact that people have free will is incompatible with the racist notion that character is determined by genetic lineage. He will discover that character is a matter not of a person's blood or heritage, but of a person's choices and actions. He will come to judge people not as cogs of a collective, but as autonomous individuals. And by thus deriving his beliefs logically from facts, he will foster harmony between his emotions and reality. He might even end up marrying someone of a different race whom his prior irrationality would have disqualified at first sight.

Healthy emotions are those that are in harmony with the facts of reality, and such emotions are products of rational, observation-based, non-contradictory thinking.

Of course, reason does not make us infallible; we can err in our thinking. Consequently, we can draw false conclusions that, in turn, lead to conflicting emotions. But the only way to correct a false idea is by looking at the facts and logically reassessing them until we discover the truth of the matter. If we use reason *consistently*— as a matter of *principle*—then, over time, true ideas displace false ones, and our feelings come into harmony with the facts. (Note, in this regard, that while most children go through a stage during which they scream and cry when others won't share their belongings with them, most adults no longer suffer this spiritual conflict—because they have come to recognize the principle of property rights.)

Now, it is important to remember that our emotions are themselves facts—facts that are extremely relevant to our life and well-being. Thus, our emotions should not be ignored or repressed. Like all relevant facts, they should be acknowledged and properly considered. But just as the existence and relevance of our lungs does not render them our means of knowledge, so the existence and relevance of our emotions does not grant *them* that role.

Our emotions are crucially important to our life and happiness, but they are *not* our means of knowledge. They do not tell us what is true or false; thus, they cannot tell us what is good or bad, right or wrong. Only reason can. We recognize the truth of this principle every time we feel like taking one course of action but then consider the facts, use logic, and realize that another course would be better.

If we want to live and enjoy life, we have to respect each of our mental faculties for what it is. Reason is our means of knowledge; it is our basic means of achieving our values and living. Emotions are consequences of our ideas; they are our psychological means of experiencing our values and enjoying life. With these principles in mind, let us turn to our next subject: how to make life meaningful.

5

Making Life Meaningful
Living Purposefully

In Chapter 4, we saw the life-or-death importance of productive work and, more fundamentally, of rational thinking. We also discovered what emotions are and how they come to be. Finally, we observed and contrasted the crucial yet distinct roles of reason and emotion in human life and happiness. We will now capitalize on these truths. In this chapter, we turn to the question of how to make life meaningful. And the key word here is: make.

Life does not come with ready-made meaning; we are not born with pre-packaged purpose. If we want our life to be meaningful, we have to *make it so.*

Our life is a process of self-generated, goal-directed action—action that, because we have free will, is generated by us toward goals *chosen* by us. The meaning of our life is a function of the goals we choose to pursue—that is, our purposes.

A *purpose* is a conscious, intentional goal—a goal chosen and pursued for a desired outcome. A *rational* purpose is a purpose that promotes one's life—such as getting an education, developing a career, engaging in a hobby, building a romantic relationship, or raising one's children. These are the kinds of goals that make life meaningful.

For example, consider a college student who chooses his major carefully, goes to class regularly, and takes his studies seriously. He is selfishly *after* something; he is acting purposefully toward a life-promoting end. In so doing, he adds meaning to his life in the form of value-achievements—such as increased knowledge, improved judgment, and an earned diploma. By contrast, consider a college student who picks a major at random, frequently skips class to "hang out" in the coffee shop, and studies just enough to "get by." He is *not* selfishly after anything; he is not acting purposefully toward a life-promoting end. Consequently, he achieves nothing of value; he adds no meaning to his life. Even if he happens to receive a diploma, it will be meaningless, because he did not put anything into it; he did not *earn* it. Meaningful values are products of purposeful efforts. They have to be earned.

In regard to career, suppose a young office clerk decides that he wants to manage the company for which he works. He commits himself to learning everything he can about the business, constantly asks himself what can be done to improve operations, develops innovative ideas, presents them to his superiors, and seizes every opportunity to excel. Not surprisingly, over the course of some interesting, action-packed years, he makes his way to the top—where he does not stop: Once there, he strives to take the company to ever greater heights. Here is a person acting purposefully and, as a result, making his days and years exciting, inspiring, and rewarding—filling his life with meaning.

Now, contrast him to a young office clerk with the same potential, but who sets no such goals, takes no such actions, and stagnates as a clerk for the rest of his life. What will be the meaning of his days and years? What spiritual values will he achieve by means of his lethargy? The answer is obvious.

The meaning of one's life is determined by the choices one makes and the effort one exerts. Whether one's life is meaningful or meaningless depends on whether or not one chooses to be rational and purposeful.

Of course, irrational choices and actions may be said to have negative meaning—in that they have anti-life consequences. But this does not grant them any moral validity. Taking life-destroying actions is not a means to an "alternative lifestyle." Acting against one's life and long-term happiness is not another way to live; it is only a way to die.

Observe further, in this connection, that there is no such thing as a "neutral" goal or value. Since the hours and days of life are limited and irretrievable, for a person to spend any time doing something that is not good for his life is to act in a manner that is *bad* for his life. There is no middle ground here. Life is finite, and time is irreplaceable; thus, for a person to do something that does not advance his life *is* to retard his life. Since any of his misplaced effort of the past could have gone toward furthering his life but did not, his life at present is rendered less meaningful than it would otherwise have been. As to instances of non-effort: If rather than having idled a person had pursued a life-promoting goal or value, his life would correspondingly have become more meaningful.

For instance, if a person complacently settles into a job that he does not enjoy—and makes no effort to find or create one that he does enjoy—he cuts himself off from life as it might and ought to be. Similarly, if he sits around channel surfing all weekend, he forgoes countless alternative activities by means of which he could have made his life interesting and meaningful. Likewise, if he stays up all night getting mindlessly drunk, he misses out on the sleep he otherwise could have gotten, which would have enabled him to do something productive or exciting the next day.

Those who do not choose to pursue rationally purposeful, life-promoting values, lead spiritually meaningless, value-empty lives. Granted, their default renders them without *emotional* grounds for comparison; so they might not *feel* that they are missing anything. But this does not change the fact that they are missing out on life. Nor does it change the fact that there are *rational* grounds for comparison—such as those we are discussing here. So, regardless of whether they feel that they are missing out on anything, they still have the ability to *know* it—and to *do* something about it. Of course, the choice is theirs to make; boring or interesting, miserable or joyful, their life belongs to them.

Fortunately, they do not own your life or mine.

We live once. Every moment matters. Every effort counts. Every choice has a consequence. There are no neutral goals or values, because every choice we make either promotes our life or retards it. If we want to live our life to the fullest, we have to recognize this fact and act accordingly.

Consider an example in the realm of romance. Compare a rational man who is intent on building a long-term love-filled relationship with a woman—to a playboy who chooses to sleep with as many women as he can. The rational man's relationship expands, deepens, and becomes fuller each day. Consequently, when he and his lover make love, it is not only a physical pleasure, but also a highly *spiritual* one; it is filled with all the knowledge, memories, and values that he and his lover share and revere. The playboy's "relationships," on the other hand, are empty. He shares *no* significant memories or values with his partners; he never even gets to know one woman before he's on to the next. Consequently, his sexual escapades have no spiritual value; they are engagements of mere friction. Meaningful sex is a function of a meaningful relationship, and such a relationship requires a rationally purposeful approach.

The point here is that, as human beings, we have physical *and* spiritual needs; and if we want to live and achieve happiness, we have to identify and satisfy *both*.

Take an example in the field of parenting. Consider a mother who embraces the responsibility of properly raising her children, works hard to discover and employ the principles of good parenting, and strives to be the best mother she can be. She sets a good example for her children, teaches them the importance and joys of choosing and pursuing rational goals, encourages them to ask questions, and talks with them regularly about their thoughts and feelings. In so doing, she fosters their spiritual growth and helps them to become independent, self-confident, life-loving adults. Consequently, her children and her relationships with them add great meaning to her life.

Compare her to a mother who neglects her maternal responsibilities, makes no effort to discover the principles of good parenting, and raises her kids by the "seat of her pants." She sets a bad example for them, teaches them nothing of the importance or joys of rational goals, discourages their question-asking, and disregards their ideas and feelings. Does she foster their spiritual growth—or does she hinder it? And what is the consequence of this? Will her children add great meaning to her life—or will they be a source of strife and resentment? Again, the answer is clear.

Of course, since people have free will, her children might still choose to think and exert the effort necessary to become independent, self-confident, life-loving adults. But if they do, it will be no thanks to their selfless, irrational mother; rather, it will be a tribute solely to their own selfish use of reason.

The principle is: If we want our life to be meaningful, we have to be rationally purposeful; we have to choose and pursue rational goals in each major area of our life: work, romance, friendship, recreation, and (if we choose to have children) parenting.

Let us now turn to a narrower principle pertaining to this issue. In order to succeed in pursuing our purposes, we must choose goals and values that are *compatible* with one another. We cannot develop a career if another interest keeps pulling us away from it, or enjoy a hobby that we can't afford, or build a romantic relationship if we have no time. In order to accomplish our goals fully and harmoniously, we need to organize them around a central goal by reference to which we can combine our efforts into a unified, meaningful, robust life. Such a goal is what Ayn Rand called a *central purpose.*

> A central purpose serves to integrate all the other concerns of a man's life. It establishes the hierarchy, the relative importance, of his values, it saves him from pointless inner conflicts, it permits him to enjoy life on a wide scale and to carry that enjoyment into any area open to his mind.[1]

A person's central purpose (if he has selected one) is his primary long-range goal in life. This goal is by definition more important than his secondary or short-range goals; thus, it takes precedence over them. This does not mean that he shouldn't have other concerns or interests; it simply means that if he wants to live his life to the fullest—if he wants to make the most of his days and years—he has to prioritize his goals and pursue them accordingly. Logically, his most important goal should get the greatest degree of his attention.

---

1. Ayn Rand, interview by Alvin Toffler, *Playboy,* March 1964.

What qualifies as a central purpose? Any long-range productive goal—so long as one makes it primary and takes it seriously. It has to be a *productive* goal, because of the central role of productive work in human life—the fact that one either produces or dies (or becomes a parasite). And it ought to be something one *loves* to do, because, while life is the standard of value, the moral purpose of one's life is the achievement of one's happiness. Thus, in short: One's central purpose should be a long-range productive goal toward which one loves to work.

Usually, one's central purpose is one's career; however, it can be broader than that. For example, a person might choose the relatively specific goal of mastering the art of teaching history to high-school students, or he might decide on the more general goal of seeking excellence as an educator in the field of history. Whereas the first would probably include just one career, the second could subsume a number of different careers: He could begin by teaching at the high-school level, then become a college professor, later turn to writing textbooks, and still later produce historical documentaries.

Either way, whether narrow or broad, a person's central purpose enables him to evaluate and coordinate all of his other concerns in life. It enables him to ask himself: Given my main mission, will this course of action add to or detract from my life and long-term happiness? If it will add to my life, where in the hierarchy of my values does it belong? How does it fit in with my other goals? How much of my time and energy should it get? And so forth. A person's central purpose enables him to take control of his life, to manage it effectively, and to fill it with meaning.

Of course, since life is replete with interesting possibilities, opportunities, and alternatives, one's central purpose might change over time. For instance, a woman might spend the first half of her adult life dedicated to building and running a semiconductor company, and then move to the countryside and devote her time and energy to painting landscapes. Another woman might choose to have children and commit a substantial number of years to raising them properly—during which time her central purpose would be motherhood—and later, after her children are grown, open an advertising agency. Yet another person might study dentistry and practice it for a number of years, then decide to sell the business and make his primary concern some activity that previously was just a hobby, say, woodworking.

In any case, if one wants to fill one's life with meaning and joy, one needs a central purpose by reference to which one can organize and prioritize one's values. It may be narrow or broad; it may subsume a single or several careers; and it may change over time. But if one wants to live as a human being and achieve genuine happiness, one has to choose and pursue a rational, selfish, life-promoting central purpose of some kind or another.

In a specialized society, the possibilities from which to choose are seemingly endless. One can be a scientist, a chef, a conductor, a Marine, a philosopher, a truck driver, a brain surgeon, or a fisherman. One can grow flowers, practice law, build bridges, paint portraits, play baseball, direct movies, sell insurance, or fly airplanes. One can make a central purpose of almost any interest—so long as it involves some sort of rational, productive work; and, importantly, it should be work one loves to do.

To support oneself by pursuing the goals one rationally loves to pursue is to enjoy one's life by embracing the requirements of living as a human being. This is the moral ideal—the essence of good living—and to achieve it, one must simultaneously gain and maintain yet another spiritual value, one closely related to reason and purpose, namely: self-esteem.

Self-esteem is the dual conviction that one is *able* to live and *worthy* of happiness.[2] Its two components, self-confidence and self-respect, are objective requirements of human life and happiness. If a person does not develop self-confidence, he will not be able to live successfully, because he will have no psychological motivation to put forth the necessary effort. Why should he try if he cannot succeed? And if a person does not develop self-respect, he will not be able to achieve happiness, because he will lack the positive personal evaluation that is the *essence* of happiness. How can he be happy if he thinks he is no good?

While self-esteem is essential to human life and happiness, people are not born with it; they have to *earn* it. And the only

---

2. See Rand, *For the New Intellectual,* p. 128; and Peikoff, *Objectivism,* p. 306.

way to earn it is by means of rational achievement. A person comes to believe that he is worthy of happiness by using his mind and striving to succeed in life. And he comes to believe that he is able to live by exerting effort and accomplishing life-serving goals. To the extent he believes that he can deal with the world and that he deserves to be happy, he is psychologically positioned for success. To the degree he believes that he cannot deal with the world or that he does not deserve to be happy, he is psychologically positioned for failure.

Thus, self-esteem is as important to human life and happiness as are reason and purpose; and there is only one way to gain or keep it: by thinking rationally and acting purposefully. This is why *reason, purpose,* and *self-esteem* are, as Ayn Rand explained, "the three values which, together, are the means to and the realization of one's ultimate value, one's own life."[3]

To live as human beings we have to think (reason); we have to choose and pursue life-promoting goals (purpose); and we have to achieve and maintain the conviction that we are able to live and worthy of happiness (self-esteem). All three are necessary for success in every area of our life.

To underscore the importance of these values, consider one of the great rewards for upholding them: romantic love. In the full sense of the term, romantic love is possible only to a person who thinks rationally, pursues life-serving purposes, and cultivates self-esteem. To understand why, we need only ask a few questions.

With respect to reason: How could a couple communicate with each other, plan a future together, or settle disagreements if one of them placed emotions or feelings *over* rational judgment and facts? Imagine pointing out the facts regarding an important issue and rationally explaining to your lover why you are taking a certain position, and then hearing him or her say: "I'm not swayed by facts or reason—my feelings tell me what's right and wrong." How long would that relationship last?

As to purpose: How could a person be romantically attracted to someone who has no creative interests, goals, or ambition? In other words, how attractive is a couch potato? Could you fall or

---

3. Rand, "The Objectivist Ethics," p. 27.

remain in love with a person who does not want to be productive or accomplish anything? Conversely, if you had no passion for achievement would you expect anyone to love you?

Regarding self-esteem: If a person is not worthy of his own love, how can he be worthy of another's? What on earth could someone else know about his character that he doesn't know? Would you want to become romantically involved with a person who—by his or her *own* conviction—is just no good? And how could a person who does not love himself love anyone else anyway? With what "self" would he love them? As Howard Roark, the hero of Ayn Rand's novel *The Fountainhead,* so eloquently put it: "To say 'I love you' one must know first how to say the 'I.'"

Reason, purpose, and self-esteem are the basic human values—the fundamental values on which our life and happiness depend. If we want to live and make the most of our life—if we want to fill our life with meaning—we have to uphold these values consistently, without compromise, as a matter of principle. How to do so is the subject of Chapter 6.

6

Objective Moral Virtues

Principled Actions

Having considered the basic values on which human life depends, we now turn to the question of *virtue*. While a moral value is an *object* (or thing) by means of which one promotes one's life, a moral virtue is an *action* (or choice) by means of which one does so.[1] Thus, we actually have been discussing virtue for some time: The faculty of reason is a value—the act of thinking is a virtue; one's career is a value—productive work is a virtue; self-esteem is a value—acting to gain and keep it is a virtue.

Generally speaking, since man's life is the standard of moral value, the kinds of actions that promote his life are virtues; the kinds of actions that harm or destroy it are vices. As Ayn Rand put it: "Since reason is man's basic means of survival, that which is proper to the life of a rational being is the good; that which negates, opposes or destroys it is the evil."[2] The moral status of an action is determined by reference to this principle.

Virtues are the basic types of actions proper to the life of a rational being; thus, they are discovered and validated by reference to the nature and requirements of human life. Since human life occurs over a span of years and decades, a virtue must account not only for the present, but also for the more distant future. And

---

1. Cf. Rand, *For the New Intellectual,* p. 121.
2. Rand, "The Objectivist Ethics," p. 25.

since we are complex beings of body and mind, a virtue must account not only for our physical needs (such as food, clothing, and shelter), but also for our spiritual needs (such as self-esteem, friendship, and love).

In Chapter 5, we briefly considered the principle that in order to make the most of our life, we have to organize our values hierarchically (according to their relative importance) and pursue them with respect to that hierarchy. Put negatively, this principle means that we must never commit a *sacrifice;* we must never surrender a greater value for the sake of a lesser one.[3] Of course, life requires that we regularly forgo lesser values for the sake of greater ones. But these are gains, not sacrifices. A sacrifice consists in giving up something that is *more* important for the sake of something that is *less* important; thus, it results in a net loss.

Consider some obvious examples. If a collector of baseball cards trades one that means more to him for one that means less, he has committed a sacrifice. If he trades one that means less for one that means more, he has achieved a gain, not incurred a loss. Similarly, if a student has a test in the morning that bears heavily on his long-term well-being, then it is not a sacrifice to put off watching his favorite television show in order to study. The importance of doing well on the test outweighs the pleasure he would get from watching TV; thus, if he were to watch the show instead of studying, *that* would be a sacrifice. Likewise, if a happily married man finds himself sexually attracted to a woman other than his wife, it is not a sacrifice for him to abstain from pursuing an affair with her. On the contrary, it would be a sacrifice to pursue the affair: These values—his wife, his marriage, his integrity, and his self-esteem—are enormously important; to surrender them for the sake of meaningless sex would be an immense loss. (If a man becomes unhappy in his marriage, he should take rational action to remedy the problem, such as seeking counseling or getting a divorce.)

Virtue is a matter of logic. Just as logic is one's method for checking the validity of one's ideas, so it is one's method for

---

3. See Rand, "The Ethics of Emergencies," in *The Virtue of Selfishness,* p. 50.

checking the propriety of one's actions. With regard to ideas, the standard is *evidence* and the principle is *non-contradiction*. With regard to actions, the standard is *the hierarchy of one's values* and the principle is *non-sacrifice*. In each case, the principle entails consistency with the rational standard. The first regards allegiance to reality and its laws; the second regards loyalty to the requirements of one's life.

Is a given *idea* consistent with what one knows by way of evidence to be true? Does it fit without contradiction into the network of one's observation-based knowledge? If so, it is valid; if not, it is not. Is a given *action* consistent with the hierarchy of one's values? Will it promote rather than sacrifice one's life and long-term happiness? If so, it is proper; if not, it is not.

If one's ideas are to serve one's life and happiness, one must accept only rational, observation-based, non-contradictory ideas; and one must reject all others. Likewise, if one's actions are to serve one's life and happiness, one must choose only rational, life-promoting, non-sacrificial actions; and one must refuse all others. In order to live one's life to the fullest, one must integrate one's ideas, convictions, and values into a non-contradictory, non-sacrificial, *unified* whole; and one must act accordingly—as a matter of principle.

We have seen that rational thinking and productive work are our two most basic action requirements. By our nature, we have to think and produce in order to live and prosper. Thus, rationality and productivity are major virtues. And since rational thinking guides productive work, not vice versa, rationality is the more fundamental of the two. In fact, since thinking is the most basic chosen action underlying and making possible *all* of our life-promoting activities, rationality is the *primary* moral virtue.

Rationality is "the recognition and acceptance of reason as one's only source of knowledge, one's only judge of values and one's only guide to action."[4]

If we want to live, we have to think, judge, and act rationally; but this is a very broad concept, and to make practical use of it in everyday life, we need narrower, more specific guidelines. Enter

---

4. Rand, "The Objectivist Ethics," pp. 27–28.

the derivative virtues of productivity, honesty, integrity, independence, justice, and pride. Each of these is an application of rationality to a specific aspect of life. By considering each of them, we will advance our understanding of the nature of virtue and thereby increase our ability to achieve our life-serving values and happiness.

Productivity (or productiveness) "is the process of creating material values, whether goods or services."[5] Since we have already seen the fundamental importance of this virtue, we will not spend much time on it here. Suffice it to say that a person either produces the values required to sustain and further his life, or he dies. Of course, if other people are willing to serve as his host, he can exist as a parasite. But this is not a third alternative; it is merely a version of the second. To borrow the words of psychologist Edwin A. Locke: "There are two kinds of dead people: the dead-dead and the living-dead." Psychologically speaking, people who are parasites are not alive (which is why they are so boring to talk to). For human beings, living consists in thinking, creating, and enjoying the fruits of one's own efforts. Productiveness is *central* to the process. This is why, as we have seen, productive work is properly one's central purpose in life: It makes life both possible and interesting.

In short, productiveness is a virtue by nature of the fact that human values do not come ready-made in nature; if we want to live and achieve happiness, we have to produce the material values on which our life and happiness depend. Recognition of this fact is simply a matter of honesty, which is our next virtue.

Honesty "is the refusal to fake reality—i.e., to pretend that facts are other than they are."[6] It can be described as the flip side of rationality: Whereas rationality is the commitment to think, judge, and act with respect to the relevant facts, honesty is the commitment *not* to do otherwise.

Since reality remains what it is regardless of any efforts to ignore or deny it—since facts are facts and cannot be wished away—the consequences of recognizing reality can only be positive, and

---

5. Peikoff, *Objectivism,* p. 292.
6. Ibid., p. 267.

the consequences of evading it can only be negative. The following examples will bear this out.

Generally speaking, a job applicant who presents his actual qualifications, and does not pretend to possess qualities he does not have, will be able to perform his responsibilities successfully if he is hired. Thus, he will likely be retained and might even be promoted. But an applicant who misrepresents his qualifications, by pretending to possess qualities he does not have, will be unable to perform his responsibilities successfully if *he* is hired. Consequently, he might be demoted but more likely will be fired.

Similarly, if a married man maintains fidelity to his wife, and lives his life rationally in all other regards as well, he will know that he is a faithful husband and a good person. Consequently, he will be able to respect himself and enjoy his marriage—which, due to his honesty, will be intact. By contrast, if a married man cheats on his wife, regardless of whatever else he does, he will know that he is a lying adulterer. Thus, he will be unable to respect himself or enjoy his marriage—which, due to his dishonesty, will be in tatters.

Of course, there can be circumstances in which an extramarital affair does not involve dishonesty. For instance, if a woman's husband is in a coma for some length of time and she loses all hope of his recovery, falls in love with another man, and decides to move on with her life, she is hardly dishonest for doing so. Likewise, if a married man wants to divorce his wife but she or the government will not allow him to do so, it is not dishonest of him to have an affair with another woman. Nor is a person being dishonest if he has an extramarital relationship to which he, his spouse, and the third party agree. Such choices and actions are not dishonest, because they do not entail the pretense that facts are other than they are.

Brief and straightforward examples about honesty versus dishonesty can be multiplied end over end, but there is more involved here than such examples can reveal. To better understand the meaning and implications of honesty, we need to consider a few examples in greater detail and from several perspectives.

Let us compare the life of an honest bank manager to that of a dishonest one. The honest manager acknowledges his commitments, works hard, reconciles his books, and refuses to take money that does not belong to him. Thus, he is able to face his associates and customers with a clear conscience—knowing that he is doing a good job, upholding his chosen obligations, and treating everyone fairly. Further, since he has nothing to hide, he is able to talk about his work to his family and friends without having to worry about what he says or to whom he says it. Whether at work, home, or play, he is able to live his life openly and fearlessly with no need to "cover his tracks." By being honest, he is living in *harmony* with reality and reaping the consequent rewards.

The dishonest manager takes a different course of action. He "cooks" his books and embezzles from his customers. He is acting in *conflict* with reality—that is, *against* the fact that he does not own the money he is taking. Consequently, he has big problems. Besides the fact that he might get caught and thrown in jail for embezzlement, in order to maintain the illusion of his innocence he will have to engage in additional acts of dishonesty to cover up the initial one. Then he will have to tell even more lies to cover up the cover-up lies, and so on. Each act of dishonesty will necessitate further lies in an ever-expanding web of deceit. The following are, in pattern, just some of the kinds of lies he will have to tell as a result of his one act of dishonesty.

If his family or friends ask about the nature of his financial "success," he will have to lie to them about it. If he tells them that he got a raise, he had better hope they never run into his boss and mention the alleged achievement. If they do, the liar will then have to lie to his boss about why he lied to his family and friends about getting a raise; and he will have to lie to his family and friends about why his boss claimed to know nothing of it. If, instead, he tells his family and friends that he is working a second job, he had better hope they don't ask "Where?" If they do, he will have to tell them *something.* If he makes up a company, he had better hope they don't try to contact him there. If they do, he will have to lie about why the company is "unlisted" or "top se-cret" or something like that. If, instead, he names an existing com-pany, he had better hope they don't call looking for him *there.* If they do, he will have to lie about why the receptionist has never heard of him. If he knows the receptionist, and if she is willing to lie for him by also pretending that he works where he does not, he will be at her mercy thereafter—and we already know the nature of *her* character. If over the course of his cover-up efforts he tells different lies to different people (as he will have to do), he had better hope they never communicate with one another about anything having to do with him. If they do, he will have to lie again to all of them about why he lied to the others. And so forth.

Each new lie will require the dishonest manager to tell additional lies in order not to get caught in his previous lies. Of course, there is no way to predict the *specific* lies he will have to tell, since they will depend on the particular circumstances surrounding his various attempts at deception. But what *is* certain is that if he wants to avoid exposure, he will have to lie again and again. What is also certain is that he will not be able to escape the consequence of his dishonesty: self-destruction.

Until and unless the dishonest manager decides to change his ways, atone for his wrongdoings, and start doing what is right, each lie he tells will further chip away at any remnant of self-esteem that might be left within him. And he will be lying more often than one might suspect. He will be lying *a lot*. He will be lying to his customers when he tells them that their money is in "good hands" (chip . . .); to his subordinates when he reminds them of his alleged standards (chip . . .); to his boss when she asks, "How go the books, Joe?" (chip . . .); to his date when *she* asks, "What do you like most about your career, Joe?" (chip . . .); to his friends when they marvel at his "lifestyle" (chip . . .); to his future employer about his past "performance" (chip . . .); even to the grocer when he exchanges a dollar he does not rightfully own for a banana he does not actually deserve (chip . . .).

The point is twofold: 1) Dishonesty cannot be contained, and 2) its effects cannot be escaped. Once a person begins lying, his dishonesty spreads like cancer throughout his life, creating anxiety and destroying his self-esteem. While he might not get physically "caught," his need to continuously "cover his tracks" combined with his irrepressible knowledge of the fact that he is a fraud will spiritually thwart every significant aspect of his life.

Just as a person cannot wish facts out of existence, so he cannot wish knowledge out of his mind. He cannot expel what he knows to be true. He *can* ignore or evade his knowledge—that's precisely what dishonesty *is*—but he cannot get rid of it. He cannot un-know what he knows. Reality won't let him.

Until and unless a dishonest person stops lying, makes appropriate reparations, and commits himself to being honest, he will continue to destroy himself, lie by lie, chip by chip.

Another telling angle on the vice of dishonesty is that it puts a person in the position of relying on peoples' *inability* to discover the facts surrounding his so-called life. While to an honest person, a friend or colleague's keen eye and good judgment provide a benefit—to a dishonest person, these same qualities pose a threat. A dishonest person has to surround himself with people whom he can deceive, and he has to avoid those whom he cannot. In other words, his character trait of choice in others is their gullibility. The only people who qualify for partnership, friendship, or romance with him are those whom he, a degenerate, can delude. As Ayn Rand put it, a dishonest person is "a dependent on the stupidity of others . . . a fool whose source of values is the fools he succeeds in fooling."[7]

That fact alone speaks volumes. But there's more.

Perhaps the most revealing fact of all regarding the selflessness of dishonesty is that the time and energy a dishonest person puts into deceiving the deceivable could have gone into achieving the achievable. It could have gone toward creating values rather than fooling people. It could have gone toward promoting his life rather than retarding it—which is all that dishonesty can do.

If a person attempts to gain a value by means of dishonesty, even if he appears to "get away" with it, he actually does not. The ill-gotten gain does not and cannot bring him happiness; it necessarily creates spiritual conflict, anxiety, and self-contempt. Since he was dishonest to *get* the "value," he will have to continue being dishonest to *keep* it. And since he knows that he gained the "value" dishonestly, he also knows that he is not worthy of having it. Consequently, the "value" cannot serve its intended purpose; it cannot promote his life; thus, it is not—in the moral, life-

---

7. Rand, *For the New Intellectual*, p. 129.

serving sense of the term—a value. It is a *dis*value; it can only thwart his life and work against his happiness.

To understand why this is so, we must bear in mind the fact that a person can value something that is *not* in his best interest. He can act to gain or keep things that harm or destroy his life— such as an abusive spouse or a heroin "high." And we must acknowledge that, morally speaking, such things are not legitimate values, because they do not and cannot promote human life; they can only harm or destroy it.

In the broadest, goal-directed sense of the term, a value is anything that one acts to gain or keep. But in the narrower, moral sense of the term, a legitimate value is a value that actually promotes one's life.[8]

For instance, if a person earns money and buys a car with it, the car is a legitimate value; it can promote his life, and he can enjoy driving it. His possession of the car is a result of his virtue; thus, it is a reward and a reminder of his accomplishments. But if a person steals a car, the car is *not* a legitimate value; it cannot promote his life, and he literally cannot enjoy driving it—not unless chronic fear and self-doubt are the hallmarks of joy. His possession of the car is a result of his vice; thus, it is a penalty in the form of a reminder that he is a thief. In addition to the fact that he might get caught and thrown in jail for stealing the car, driving it will always remind him that he is a parasite, and anything he uses the car to "accomplish" will be tainted by that fact. If he picks up a deceivable date, even though she may not know it, *he* will know that she is getting into someone *else's* car with an incompetent who can't earn money to buy his own. Likewise, if strangers admire the car, the thief will know that they are admiring someone *else's* hard-earned accomplishment, which he (the thief) could only muster the "guts" to steal.

Now, the thief might *say* that he is enjoying the car. But his words cannot reverse cause and effect. Genuine joy comes from *achieving* values, not from stealing them. Happiness is an *effect*— of which personal achievement is the *cause.* No one—no matter

---

8. Cf. Leonard Peikoff, *Unity in Epistemology and Ethics,* taped lecture (New Milford: Second Renaissance Books, 1997).

how stupid he might be—can make himself "believe" that he has achieved something when he *knows* that he has not. The one person no one can fool, in this respect, is oneself.

Dishonesty cannot lead to values. Reality won't let it.

To further illustrate this point, consider a student who cheats on an exam. Even if he does not get caught and expelled from school, the cheating cannot promote his life. For starters, since higher-level knowledge is built on lower-level knowledge, if he has not learned how to write a sentence or do arithmetic, how will he learn to write a paragraph or do algebra? And if he cannot write a paragraph or do algebra, how will he ever write an essay or do calculus? He won't. Like the book-cooking bank manager, he will have to cheat again to cover up his initial cheating, and then again to cover up that cheating, and so on. And like the car-stealing incompetent, if the cheating "gets" him a "good" grade, since he will know that he did not *earn* it, every "accomplishment" built thereon will be spoiled by his irrepressible knowledge of the fact that he is not an achiever but a deceiver.

For instance, if his cheating gets him into a college, then in addition to being ill-equipped to do the necessary schoolwork, he will know that he does not deserve to be there in the first place. If he continues cheating throughout college and that gets him into a law school, then in addition to being ill-equipped to do his coursework, he will know that he does not deserve to be there, either. If he persists and cheats his way through law school and into a law firm, then in addition to being ill-equipped to do his casework, he will know that his entire "career" is built on a pile of sham. What kind of life will he then have? Will he be genuinely happy? Or will he be spiritually eaten by his knowledge of the fraud that he actually is?

Dishonesty is incompatible with life and happiness for the simple reason that it pits a person against the very source and realm of values: reality.

Morality is a matter of the immutable laws of identity, causality, and non-contradiction. An action either promotes a person's life and long-term happiness, or it does not. If it does, it is virtuous; if it does not, it is not. For someone to "get away" with being dishonest—for dishonesty to "promote" a person's life—would literally take a miracle: a violation of natural law. In other words: It can't happen.

Ill-gotten gains are not and cannot be values; they are and can only be *dis*values. They are not rewards, but penalties. They do not promote one's life; they thwart it—and they do so every time. Thus, not only is it true that honesty pays; the deeper truth is that *only* honesty pays. Such is the nature of reality.

In the above examples, the acts of honesty and dishonesty are rather obvious. But the requirements of honesty are not always so easy to discern. Consider another kind of situation.

Suppose a robber walks into a store, points a gun at the owner, and demands: "Empty your cash drawer into this bag, or I'll blow your head off!" Fearing for his life, the owner complies. The robber then demands to know if there is any more money on the premises. Here is the tricky part: Since the owner keeps a few hundred dollars hidden in the back room, is he morally obligated to inform the thief of this fact—or can he lie and still maintain his honesty?

To answer such a question we must bear in mind the *purpose* of morality. The purpose of morality is to guide a person in living as a human being. The purpose of moral principles is to guide a human being in gaining and keeping his life-serving values. Thus, in order for a moral principle to be *valid*, it has to serve that purpose. With this in mind, we can begin to answer the question.

For a person to be able to *keep* his values, he must also be able to *protect* them from people who wish to steal, harm, or destroy them. And for honesty to be a virtue, it has to allow for such protection. Thus, honesty cannot mean "never, under any circumstance, tell a lie"; it cannot be the virtue of "always telling the truth, no matter what the consequence." Such a "virtue" would not permit a person to protect his life-serving values; thus, it would defeat the very purpose of morality.

If honesty required a person to "always tell the truth no matter what," it would be opposed to life; in other words, it would not be a virtue. What honesty *does* require a person to do is to account for *all* of his knowledge—and to ignore or evade *none* of it.

Honesty means *never faking reality in order to gain a value.* It is the virtue of refusing to pretend that facts are other than they are. As such, it requires recognition of *all* the relevant facts of a given situation—and *only* the facts.

Given the purpose of morality, honesty *does* permit a person to lie—*if* the lie is intended to protect a legitimate value from a person (or group) who seeks to steal, harm, or destroy it.

Thus, unless the storeowner has reason to believe that doing so would further endanger his life, lying to the thief would *not* be an act of dishonesty. On the contrary, it would be an act of honesty. He would be accounting for *all* the facts and *only* the facts—including the fact that his money is rightfully his—and excluding the fiction (the non-fact) that the thief has any right to take it.

Honesty requires that one take into account the *full context* of one's knowledge. Dishonesty consists in ignoring or evading *some aspect* of one's knowledge. In attempting to steal the storeowner's money, the thief is trying to gain a value that is *not* rightfully his by ignoring this and other relevant facts. In lying to the thief, the storeowner is trying to keep a value that *is* rightfully his by acknowledging this and all the relevant facts. The thief is placing his fantasy over reality; the storeowner is placing nothing over reality.

Whether one should tell the truth or not depends on the context of the situation in question. Lying to a friend in order to lure him to his surprise party is not a breach of morality; the context makes such a lie morally appropriate and thus perfectly honest. Nor is it dishonest to lie to a person who is unjustly prying into one's private life. If the snoop has no morally legitimate reason to be asking certain questions, one is morally entitled to answer as necessary to thwart his unwarranted inquiry.

The broader point here is that morality is not a matter of categorical imperatives or contextless commandments. Rather, it is a matter of *purposeful principles* and *contextual absolutes:* principles formed for the purpose of making human life possible—which are to be applied absolutely with regard to the full context of one's knowledge.[9]

The full context of one's knowledge is simply the *sum* of one's knowledge—*all* of what one knows. A person is morally re-

---

9. Cf. Peikoff, *Objectivism,* pp. 274–76.

sponsible for acknowledging all the relevant items of his knowledge pertaining to any given situation with which he is faced.

Should I store the Drano in the lower cabinet or the upper one? It depends on the context: Is there a toddler in the house? Can the lower cabinet be locked? What are the surrounding facts? To ignore the context would be immoral. If my refusal to think rationally and act accordingly leads to the death of my child, I am morally responsible for his death. I am morally responsible for the consequences of my choice to be rational or irrational.

Take another situation: Should I enter the burning building or not? It depends on the context: Is someone in there? If so, who? Is it possible for me to save him—or is the building already fully engulfed in flames? What are the conditioning factors? Again, to ignore the context would be immoral. It would be quite a sacrifice to risk my life in order to save the life of a person who is clearly already dead. And it would be an even greater sacrifice to risk my life in order to save the likes of Joseph Mengele, Pol Pot, or Osama bin Laden from the flames they so richly deserve.

One more example: Should I get the money out of the drawer before I go? It depends on the context: *What* drawer? *Whose* money? What are the relevant *facts?*

You get the idea.

Questions of good and bad, right and wrong can be answered only by means of moral principles in reference to the context surrounding and conditioning the given situation. Honesty requires that we always account for that context—in full.

With this in mind, let us turn to our next virtue: integrity.

Integrity "is loyalty in action to one's convictions and values."[10] It is the virtue of walking one's talk, practicing what one preaches, living up to one's standards. In a word, it is the virtue of being *principled.*

Integrity is a matter of consistency: consistency in *thought* to that which one knows to be true, and consistency in *action* to that which one knows to be good for one's life as a rational being. It is the virtue of integrating one's convictions, values, and actions

---

10. Peikoff, *Objectivism*, p. 259.

by reference to the facts of reality and the requirements of one's life and long-term happiness.

Thus, integrity does not mean merely "acting on one's convictions." The fact that a person acts on his convictions does not *in itself* render him a man of integrity: It depends on his convictions. Are they rational, life-promoting convictions—or irrational, life-thwarting ones? Regardless of the fact that Ted Kaczynski (the "Unabomber") acted on his beliefs, he is not a man of integrity; nor was Joseph Stalin, nor Adolf Hitler, nor Timothy McVeigh, nor Mohamed Atta, nor Jack the Ripper, nor Mother Teresa. A person can have integrity only if he advocates *rational ideas* and pursues *selfish values*—ideas and values that *can* be upheld and sought consistently. Put negatively, a person cannot uphold his "standards" or be loyal to his "values" by acting against his most basic ones: life and reason.

Since a person's life is his ultimate goal, and since human life is the standard of moral value, a person who willfully acts in a manner contrary to the requirements of human life is thereby acting hypocritically; he is betraying his most fundamental choice—his choice to live. Likewise, since reason is man's means of knowledge, and thus his most essential life-serving value, a person who ignores or evades what he knows to be true is acting hypocritically; he is betraying his greatest value—his basic means of survival.

Integrity consists in loyalty to *life-promoting* values and *rational* principles—not their opposites. And it could not be otherwise: Neither irrationality nor selflessness *can* be upheld consistently; only rationality and selfishness can. A person who "believes" in placing feelings (or faith) over facts can believe it all he wants; but he cannot act on that belief consistently, or he will soon die. Merely to remain in existence he has to act rationally to some extent. For instance, he has to stop at Stop signs. Likewise, a person who "believes" in sacrificing himself for the alleged sake of others can believe it until his last breath; but he cannot act on that belief consistently, or that last breath will come quickly. Merely to stay alive, he has to act selfishly to some degree. For instance, he has to eat.

Now, it is important to bear in mind that moral virtue is not an end in itself. One does not think rationally and act selfishly in order to have integrity; one does so in order to *live*—one's ultimate goal is one's *life.* So the crucial point is not that only a rationally self-interested person can have integrity; this is true, but it is not the principle. The principle is that only a person of integrity—a person who is loyal in action to his rational convictions and values—can live and achieve genuine happiness.

A person of integrity seeks logical answers to the questions he knows to be important to his life; and he commits himself to acting rationally, in accordance with the truths he discovers. He works to keep his ideas connected to reality and to keep his actions and emotions in harmony with the facts, because he wants to live and be happy. In the event that he finds himself feeling like doing something he knows to be wrong—such as sneaking into a movie theater, cheating on an exam, or writing a bad check—he introspects to see what is causing the problem: "Why do I want to do *that?* What ideas have I accepted that are causing me to want to act against my self-interest?" In other words, he tries to identify and correct the contradiction that is causing the spiritual conflict. A person of integrity works to keep his knowledge, values, feelings, and actions *integrated.* Hence the name of the virtue.

An obvious example of a person of integrity is an employer who claims to promote his employees on the basis of their merit, and then actually does so—without exception. An employer who makes the same claim, but then occasionally promotes his employees on some other basis—such as seniority, race, gender, or "favors"—is thereby engaging in hypocrisy. What are the consequences? Since people of ability tend to prefer working for people of integrity, principled employers attract competent employees, and the hypocrites get stuck with the incompetents.

Notice that the above example is also an instance of justice versus injustice. As will become increasingly evident, all (rational) virtues imply and entail each other.

For instance, integrity requires honesty; a person of integrity never pretends that facts are other than they are. Not only does he practice what he preaches; he also preaches only what he has reason to believe is true.

To illustrate this point, consider an honest person engaged in a debate who comes to realize that his opponent's position is right and that his own position is wrong. Since he is honest, his entrance into the debate served as his word that he is actually after the truth and thus willing to concede his position if shown that it contradicts the facts. Consequently, when he discovers that he is mistaken, he acts with integrity; he admits defeat and changes his position; he discards what he now knows to be false and embraces what he now understands to be true. In so doing, he walks away from the debate having corrected his error, having gained new knowledge, and having fortified his self-esteem.

Now compare him to a dishonest person who enters into a debate intent on maintaining his position and "winning" irrespective of any logical arguments or observable facts to the contrary that his opponent might present. When the dishonest debater comes to realize that his opponent's position is right and that his own position is wrong, he hypocritically continues to assert it nonetheless. Instead of discarding the false and embracing the true, he smugly spouts such lines as: "That's only logic" or "There's more to truth than just facts" or "You're a good debater, but you're still wrong and my professor could beat you any day." Consequently, he walks away from the debate having maintained his error, having denied his own knowledge, and having lost another chunk of his self-esteem.

Which person is the better for his actions?

As the virtue of being principled, integrity requires that we monitor not only our physical actions, but also our mental ones—not only what we do with our body, but also what we do with our mind. It requires that we identify our convictions and values, and that we check the validity of the thought processes that give rise to them. Are my beliefs consistent with observable facts, or do they contradict the evidence of my senses? Are my values consistent with the requirements of my life, or do they betray that ultimate value? Did I arrive at my conclusions by means of observation and logic, or did I accept them uncritically, without a process of rational thought? Integrity requires that we check our beliefs for consistency with reality, that we check our values for consistency with the requirements of our life, and that we work to correct any contradictions we discover.

For instance, if a person acknowledges the principle that an individual's character should be judged not on the basis of his race or genetic lineage, but on the basis of his choices and actions, integrity demands that he live up to that conviction. Thus, if he finds himself advocating some practice that contradicts that principle, such as "affirmative action" or "racial quotas," integrity requires that he correct the contradiction. If he refuses—if he continues to act against what he knows in principle to be true—he is engaging in hypocrisy.

When a person of integrity discovers a contradiction in his thinking, he looks at the facts and exerts mental effort to clarify in his mind which of his conflicting ideas corresponds to reality and which does not. Then he commits himself thereafter to advocating the true idea and acting accordingly, as a matter of principle. If he discovers that neither of the ideas is true, he ceases to advocate either of them. If the issue is important, he exerts the mental effort necessary to discover what *is* the truth of the matter. Whatever the case, since he knows that he is responsible for his method of thinking, for the contents of his mind, for the actions he takes, and for his own life and happiness, he always conducts himself rationally.

Having integrity is not easy. It requires a lot of *extrospection*—the process of directing one's mental attention outward at the facts of external reality and observing the perceptual truths that are the base of one's knowledge. And it requires a great deal of *introspection*—the process of directing one's mental attention inward at the contents of one's mind (one's ideas, beliefs, values, and emotions) and monitoring the mental processes by which one acquires, holds, and experiences them. In a word, integrity requires a lot of hard mental *work*. But as Spinoza said: "All things excellent are as difficult as they are rare."

Whereas integrity is the virtue of acting in accordance with one's rational convictions and values, our next virtue, independence, pertains to the *source* of such convictions and values: one's own observation-based thinking.

Independence "is one's acceptance of the responsibility of forming one's own judgments and of living by the work of one's own mind."[11] Since we have already discussed productiveness, let us focus here on the issue of forming one's own judgments.

---

11. Rand, "The Objectivist Ethics," p. 28.

To begin, consider a person who grows up in a devoutly religious family, but then, as an adult, rejects religion on the grounds that there is neither evidence for God nor rational justification for human sacrifice. Compare him to a person from the same family who never questions the religious dogma, and thus continues to "just believe" and act selflessly for the rest of his life on the grounds that: "That's just how I was raised" or "What would people think of a selfish atheist?" The first person is relying on his own mind and his own judgment; the second is expecting others to think and judge for him. The first person is putting his own mind in first place; the second is putting the views of others in first place. The first person is an independent thinker; the second is a conformist and what Ayn Rand called a *second-hander*, because he places the views of others above and before his own perception of reality and the judgment of his own mind.

Now, a third person might reject the existence of God and the morality of sacrifice on the grounds that they are "traditional" notions accepted by other people and because he wants to be "different" or *avant-garde*. But, then, he too is a second-hander: Like the conformist, he is putting the views of others in first place; however, in his case, rather than *accepting* ideas because others do, he *rejects* ideas on that basis.

The conformist and the "non-conformist" are not fundamentally different, but fundamentally similar. Both look *to others* rather than *at reality* in order to determine what their beliefs and values should be. Neither is an independent thinker; each is a second-hander; each maintains a primary orientation toward other people, not toward reality.

An independent thinker's primary orientation is toward reality, not toward other people.[12] He is guided by the use of his *own* mind, not by the views of others. He puts his own observations and judgments in first place; he faces reality directly and deals with it *first-hand*.

An independent thinker demands rational evidence for every idea he accepts. He does not accept (or reject) ideas on the grounds that *others believe* them to be true (as do religionists, social sub-

---

12. See Peikoff, *Objectivism*, p. 251.

jectivists, and second-handers). Nor does he accept ideas just because *he wants* them to be true (as do personal subjectivists). Rather, he accepts ideas only if *he understands* them to be true—by means of his own reality-oriented, logical thinking.

If he can integrate an idea, without contradiction, into the network of his observation-based knowledge, an independent thinker accepts it; if he cannot, he does not. If he is aware of *some* evidence in support of a relevant idea, and of *no* contradictions to disqualify it, he considers the idea further but suspends his judgment until he gains sufficient evidence to draw a rational conclusion. If he later discovers that the idea entails a contradiction, he then rejects it as false. And if an idea is put forth *arbitrarily,* that is, with no supporting evidence whatsoever—such as: "*Maybe* there is a God" or "*Perhaps* some people are psychic" or "There *might* be flying monkeys on Mars"—he simply dismisses it as unworthy of his consideration, noting that to assert "maybe" is not to present *evidence.*

In sum, an independent thinker considers ideas only insofar as they are relevant to his life, are supported by some degree of evidence, and do not contradict anything he rationally knows to be true. His own logical assessment of the facts is his guide in all matters.

This is not to say that an independent thinker slights the value of experts. On the contrary, he consults them when and as needed—but always on the basis of their merit, intelligence, knowledge, ability, and character *as judged by his own mind.*

For instance, if he wants to buy a computer, he might call on an expert in the field, but not for the purpose of relinquishing his judgment on the matter. If the expert recommends a certain computer on the basis of sound reasoning, including demonstrable features and evident qualities, the independent thinker takes this advice into account. But if the alleged expert recommends a computer solely on the grounds that "Everyone who knows anything about computers is buying this one. I'm telling you—I'm an authority on computers—you don't need to look any further. This is what you want . . .," the independent thinker does not reach for his wallet.

Similarly, if he becomes ill, he might visit a doctor, but not for the purpose of blindly accepting the doctor's diagnosis or recommended treatment. Rather, he visits the doctor in order to gain knowledge so that he can make an educated decision. If the doctor's diagnosis makes sense and the suggested treatment is reasonable, the independent thinker will take them into consideration. But if the so-called doctor says, "Dude, because of a conflict in a previous life your karma is out of whack, and to realign it we'll have to perform a séance . . .," the independent thinker does not start lighting candles.

Likewise, if he hears a scientist explaining a new way in which nature can be used to lengthen or enhance human life, an independent thinker might become fascinated and begin asking questions about the discovery. But if he hears an alleged scientist preaching about the "intrinsic value" of nature, or the moral imperative of "protecting" the environment, or the looming dangers of "depleting" natural resources, an independent thinker asks himself the correspondingly appropriate questions: How can nature have "value" apart from a *valuer* and a *purpose?* Morally speaking, how can anything matter apart from its usefulness in sustaining and furthering human life? What does "protect" the environment mean? Protect it from what? *From man?* If nature is to be protected from man, how is man supposed to live? And how can natural resources be "depleted" when the world is nothing *but* natural resources? After all, what is the earth but a gigantic ball of them? And what are the other planets but a whole lot more of the same? Given a) the size of the earth, b) the immensity of the universe, and c) the fact that matter is indestructible (it can change forms but cannot go out of existence), how can we ever "run out" of resources—so long as we are free to reshape nature according to our needs? How can we ever have too little of anything—except the freedom to act on our judgment, as human life requires?

An independent thinker wants *reasons*—not appeals to "authority" or "other dimensions" or "intrinsic value." He never passively, blindly, or uncritically accepts the claims of other people. He may learn from them—if they are rational and have something to teach him. He may take their suggestions into account—if they are relevant and make sense. And he may listen to their arguments—so long as they present evidence for their claims, proceed logically, and hold human life as the standard of moral value. But he always makes the final judgment on the basis of the available evidence and by means of his own use of logic. In other words, he recognizes and accepts the fact that his own reasoning mind is his only means of gaining knowledge, judging values, or assessing claims.

There are essentially two kinds of people in the world: independent thinkers and second-handers. The first faces reality and thinks for himself; the second faces other people and expects them to think for him.

An independent thinker does not place anyone or anything above or before the judgment of his own mind, because he does not regard anything as more important than the facts of reality. Since he wants to live as a human being, to pursue his values, and to enjoy his life, he deals with reality directly, by means of his own observations and logic. When faced with a question, he looks at the facts and uses his own rational judgment to discover the truth of the matter. Since he chooses to think for himself and to form his own judgments, he is a purveyor of *spiritual* values—values such as rational ideas, self-esteem, friendship, and love. And since he chooses to support himself, to live by the work of his own mind, he is a producer of *material* values—values such as software, sculpture, skyscrapers, and medicine. In short, an independent thinker respects his psychological needs as well as his physical needs, and he does so regardless of the approval or disapproval of others. In a word, he is thoroughly *selfish.*

Not so, the second-hander. He regards the views of other people as superior to his own and as more important than the facts of reality.[13] He does not deal with reality directly, but indirectly, through other people. When faced with a question, he does not turn to the facts and use his own rational judgment to discover the truth of the matter; instead, he turns to other people to see what *they* say about it. He first wants to know what others believe, so he can then decide what he will believe. He first wants to know what others value, so he can then decide what he will value. He

---

13. See Ayn Rand, "The Argument from Intimidation," in *The Virtue of Selfishness,* p. 165 (*social metaphysician* is another, more technical term Ayn Rand used for second-hander).

first wants to know what others think, so he can then *react*—either in compliance or in defiance, depending on whether he is a conformist or a "non-conformist."

If others say that there are no absolutes, or that God exists, or that self-sacrifice is the moral ideal, or that nature must be protected, or that some smear on a canvas is a profound work of art—the second-hander does one of two things: If he is a conformist, he thoughtlessly nods his head in agreement; if he is a "non-conformist," he thoughtlessly shakes it in disagreement. Either way, he has relinquished his mind. He is not an active thinker, but a passive reactor. He is not a person on a mission, but a puppet on a string—a string held by any person or group from whom he seeks to gain or avoid approval.

In sum, being independent consists in being fact-oriented regardless of what other people think, say, or do. Put negatively, it consists in not being people-oriented in disregard of the available and relevant facts.

While independence is the virtue of maintaining one's proper relationship to reality in the presence of other people, our next virtue, justice, pertains to one's proper relationships with other people in light of reality.

Justice "is the virtue of judging men's character and conduct objectively and of acting accordingly, granting to each man that which he deserves."[14] It is the virtue of evaluating and treating people *rationally*.

The most important thing to keep in mind about other people is that, like you and I, they have free will; they *choose* the actions that form their character. They choose to think or not to think,[15] to face reality or to evade it, to act on the basis of facts or to act on the basis of feelings. This means they can be good or evil or anywhere in between—depending on their choices.

If we want to establish and maintain good relationships—relationships with good people, people conducive to our well-being—then we have to observe peoples' choices and actions, evaluate what they say and do by reference to the full context of our knowl-

---

14. Peikoff, *Objectivism*, p. 276.
15. See Rand, *For the New Intellectual*, p. 127.

edge, and treat them accordingly. This is the basic principle of selfish human interaction. And justice is the virtue of upholding this principle; it is the virtue of being rationally self-interested in regard to human relationships.

To live happily, we need to develop good relationships and avoid bad ones. We can benefit enormously from *productive* people, but not from parasites. We can trust *honest* people, but not dishonest ones. We can count on people of *integrity,* but not on hypocrites. We can learn from *independent thinkers,* but not from second-handers. In short, we can gain a great deal from those who choose to live and pursue rational, selfish values; but we can gain nothing from those who do not.

To the extent a person acts rationally (in a selfish, life-promoting manner) he is potentially, if not actually, helpful to us. To the degree a person acts irrationally (in an unselfish, life-negating manner) he is potentially, if not actually, harmful to us. Thus, if a person has any significant impact on our life, it is in our best interest to judge him accurately and treat him accordingly.

Of course, not all of our judgments of people pertain to their moral character; some pertain to other qualities such as their ability, knowledge, potential, or compatibility. For instance, we might need to know what skills a person has or how well he can perform under pressure, such as in the case of an employer evaluating a potential employee. Or we might need to know if a person is capable of teaching us anything of importance, such as in the case of a college student assessing a possible professor. Or we might need to know whether a person has sufficient interests and goals in common with us to warrant friendship or romance. But whatever the case may be—whether in regard to moral character or to other qualities—our only means of judging people is by way of reason applied to the available and relevant facts.

Note that the only other "possibilities" are our feelings (personal subjectivism) or the views of others (social subjectivism or second-handedness). Since feelings are not our means of knowledge, and since others cannot do our thinking for us, if we want to know a person's moral character or other qualities, we have to judge him *objectively*—on the basis of facts and by the use of our own mind.

Examples to validate this principle can be found wherever people interact. Take any kind of human relationship and observe the consequences therein of rational versus irrational judgment. If a businessman judges people rationally, he will be positioned to hire productive employees; if he judges people irrationally, he will find himself surrounded by incompetents, or worse. If a coach judges people rationally, he will be able to identify the strengths and weaknesses of his players; if he judges them irrationally, he will be unable to do so. If a woman seeking a romantic relationship judges people rationally, she will look for someone who is thoughtful, productive, and respectful; if she judges people irrationally, she might pursue someone who is thoughtless, parasitical, and abusive. If a teacher judges people rationally, he will be able to evaluate his students' knowledge accurately and prepare their lessons accordingly; if he judges them irrationally, he will not know what they know or what they need to learn (and God knows what he will teach them). If the dominant trend in a culture is to judge people rationally, a monster like Hitler will not get elected to the highest political office in the land; if the dominant trend is to judge people irrationally, he very well might—and did. And if the leaders of the free world judge people rationally, they will not tolerate, much less aid and abet, terrorist regimes that seek to erase freedom from the face of the earth; if they judge people irrationally, they very well might—and have.

The rational evaluation and corresponding treatment of people is an objective requirement of human life; and *moral* judgment is an essential aspect of this principle. This is why the motto "Judge not, that ye be not judged" is utterly absurd, and the moral principle to adopt in this regard is, as Ayn Rand put it: "*Judge, and be prepared to be judged.*"

> Nothing can corrupt and disintegrate a culture or a man's character as thoroughly as does the precept of *moral agnosticism,* the idea that one must never pass moral judgment on others, that one must be morally tolerant of anything, that the good consists of never distinguishing good from evil.
>
> It is obvious who profits and who loses by such a precept. It is not justice or equal treatment that you grant to men when

you abstain equally from praising men's virtues and from condemning men's vices. When your impartial attitude declares, in effect, that neither the good nor the evil may expect anything from you—whom do you betray and whom do you encourage?[16]

There is only one kind of person who has anything to fear from moral judgment; the rest of us can only benefit from it. Being just consists in acknowledging this fact and acting accordingly, without exception, as a matter of principle. In any particular case, our *means* of judging people objectively is our own use of observation-based logic; and our *standards* for doing so are the life-promoting values, principles, and virtues we are discussing here.

Finally, it is important to emphasize that justice is not primarily about condemning and punishing the bad; it is primarily about recognizing and rewarding the good. Certainly, the bad should be damned and, when necessary, retaliated against as they deserve to be and as human life requires that they be. But first and foremost, the good should be praised and, when necessary, allied with as *they* deserve to be and as human life requires that they be. This order of precedence is crucial, because it is the good who make human life possible. They are the thinkers, the producers, the creators of life-promoting values; thus, the chief concern of justice is that they be treated accordingly.

Whether a person writes the Declaration of Independence or a brilliant novel, whether he develops life-saving drugs or time-saving software, whether he makes beautiful sculptures or perfect jump-shots, whether he discovers a cure for cancer or a solution to a crucial philosophic problem—if he selfishly creates rational values, he is morally good because of it. And we who wish to live as human beings owe such people not only our candid praise and moral allegiance, but also, when appropriate, our direct thanks.

While the virtue of justice is a matter of being rationally self-interested in regard to one's relationships with other people, our next and final virtue, pride, is about being rationally self-interested in regard to one's life in general.

---

16. Ayn Rand, "How Does One Lead a Rational Life in an Irrational Society?" in *The Virtue of Selfishness,* pp. 82–83.

Pride "is the commitment to achieve one's own moral perfection."[17] As the hero of Ayn Rand's novel *Atlas Shrugged* put it: "*Pride* is the sum of all virtues."

Moral perfection is not infallibility, but an unwavering commitment to choose and pursue only selfish, life-serving values. It is not based on impossible or unachievable standards, such as "omniscience" (complete knowledge of everything) or "omnipotence" (the ability to do anything), but on the entirely possible and thoroughly achievable standard of choosing always to act on one's best judgment. Moral perfection is not the absence of mistakes, but the presence of an uncompromising commitment to living *rationally*.

To be proud is to strive to achieve one's highest potential in one's character and life. It is to be fully and consistently self-interested. It is to seek one's life-serving values with passion by resolving to use reason in every area of one's life—as a matter of principle. It is to be morally good *all* of the time. How does one do this? By actively seeking to discover what is in principle morally right, and by diligently upholding and applying the moral principles one understands to be true. In the words of Ayn Rand, one does so

> by never accepting any code of irrational virtues impossible to practice and by never failing to practice the virtues one knows to be rational—by never accepting an unearned guilt and never earning any, or, if one *has* earned it, never leaving it uncorrected—by never resigning oneself passively to any flaws in one's character—by never placing any concern, wish, fear or mood of the moment above the reality of one's own self-esteem. And, above all, it means one's rejection of the role of a sacrificial animal, the rejection of any doctrine that preaches self-immolation as a moral virtue or duty.[18]

Moral perfection *is* achievable. But it can be achieved *only* by those who accept human life as their moral standard; personal happiness as their moral purpose; and reason as their only source of knowledge, judge of values, and guide to action.

---

17. Peikoff, *Objectivism,* p. 303.
18. Rand, "The Objectivist Ethics," pp. 29–30.

Observe that while pride is commonly confused with self-deception and the refusal to stand corrected when proven wrong, such actions are logically incompatible with pride. As the commitment to achieve moral perfection, pride requires and entails *all* the moral virtues, including honesty and integrity. Thus, a proud person acknowledges his abilities and inabilities, his accomplishments and failures, his potentials and limitations; he does not attempt to deceive himself or others about who he is, what he has done, or what he can do. And he is positively *eager* to stand corrected if presented with rational evidence that is incompatible with his position, because it means the expulsion of a contradiction and the acquisition of new knowledge; it means that he is better fit to live, to pursue values, to achieve happiness.

So where does the so-called virtue of humility fit into the picture? It doesn't. Humility is belief in the notion that one is "inherently bad" or "corrupt by nature"; it is the idea that moral perfection is *impossible.* But in light of observable facts, that makes no sense at all: Human beings have free will; we *choose* the actions that shape our moral character; we are good or bad depending on the choices we make.

The idea that humility is a virtue stems from the notion that people are "inherently depraved" or "stained by original sin" or some such fiction; and just as these are myths, so is the "virtue" of humility.

Humility is not a virtue but a *vice.* It is the vice of accepting any form of the idea that one is by nature debased. It is the vice of believing oneself to be morally imperfect in the absence of any evidence to that effect. In other words, it is the vice of "just believing" or having faith that one is morally corrupt.

If a person actually does something morally wrong, he experiences not humility, but the logical consequences of his wrongdoing. For instance, if a man is dishonest with his lover, he feels rotten not because it is inherent in his nature to be dishonest, but because he *chose* to be dishonest. What is inherent in his nature is not corruption, but *free will.* Thus, if he wants to live as a human being and achieve genuine happiness, he needs to reevaluate his moral policies, correct them, and adjust his practices accordingly; he needs to start accepting only *rational* ideas and begin taking only *selfish* actions.

To contrast the virtue of pride with the vice of humility, compare two men, one of each persuasion. The man of pride recognizes that he has free will, because this fact is directly available to his mind every time he makes a choice. Since he is a man of pride, and since he knows that he chooses his values and actions, he strives always to act *rationally*—in a manner that promotes his life and happiness. Consequently, he continually gains and fortifies his self-esteem; he continually makes himself more fit to live and love life.

The man of humility, on the other hand, "just believes" that "something" about his nature "somehow" makes him "somewhat" immoral. He accepts the notion that no matter what he does, he cannot be *fully* good. But he faces this problem: He, too, knows that he has free will, because this fact is directly available to his mind every time he makes a choice. Thus, since he simultaneously *knows* that he has free will and "just believes" that he is inherently depraved, he continually deprives himself of the self-esteem he could earn if he would stop "just believing" that he is naturally corrupt and start acknowledging that his character is shaped solely by the choices he makes.

Pride is a virtue by nature of the fact that we are born neither morally good nor morally bad, but with a moral blank slate and a lifetime of choices ahead of us. The fact that we have free will means we *choose* the actions that form our character. We can choose to be good or evil or anywhere in between. But if we want to live and achieve happiness, we have to be good; and to do so, we have to discover and uphold rational, life-serving principles. If we want to make the most of our life, we have to commit ourselves to the achievement of our own moral perfection: We have to think rationally; we have to live selfishly; we have to be proud.

We have, in the preceding pages, examined the essential nature of virtue, the basic types of actions that qualify as moral. Broadly speaking, virtues are actions that support and promote our life; vices are actions that retard or destroy it. In assessing the propriety of an action, we must bear in mind not only our material needs, but also our spiritual needs—and not only for the present, but also for the more distant future. To be self-interested, we must observe reality and think; we must take into account the full context of our knowledge; we must reject contradictions; we must make life-serving value judgments; and we must act accordingly, non-sacrificially, as a matter of principle. Such are the personal requirements of a proper morality. In Chapter 7, we turn to the *social* requirements: What conditions are necessary for people to live together in a society?

7

A Civilized Society

The Necessary Conditions

We have seen that being moral consists in being self-interested—acting in a life-promoting manner. We have also seen that what most fundamentally makes life-furthering actions possible to human beings is rational thinking. In order to live, we have to use our mind to discover the requirements of our life, and we have to act accordingly. We begin this chapter with the question: What can prevent us from acting on our judgment? What can stop us from employing our means of survival?

Observe that if you are alone on an island, nothing can stop you from acting on your judgment. If you decide that you should acquire some food, you are free to make a spear and go hunting, fashion some tackle and go fishing, or plant a garden and tend to it. And if you obtain food, you are free to eat it, save it, or discard it. Likewise, if you decide that you should build a shelter, you are free to gather materials and construct one. And if you do, you are free to live in it, build an addition onto it, or tear it down. Alone on an island, you are free to act according to the judgment of your mind.

But suppose another person shows up on the island, grabs you, and ties you to a tree. Clearly, you are no longer free to act on your judgment: If you had planned to go hunting, you cannot go. If you had planned to build a shelter, you cannot build it. Whatever your plans were, they are now ruined. And if you are not freed from your bondage, you will soon die.

The brute's force has come between your planning and your acting, between your thinking and your doing. You can no longer act on your judgment; you can no longer act as your life requires; you can no longer live as a human being. Of course, the brute could feed you and keep you breathing; but a "life" of bondage is not a human life. A human life is a life guided by the judgment of one's own mind.

In order to live as human beings, we have to be *able* to act on our judgment; wild animals aside, the only thing that can stop us from doing so is *other people;* and the only way they can stop us is by using *physical force.*

Consider another example. A girl is walking to the store intent on using her money to buy some groceries when a man jumps out from an alley, points a gun at her head, and says: "Give me your purse, or die." Now the girl cannot act according to her plan. Either she is going to give her purse to the thief, or she is going to get shot in the head. In any event, she is not going grocery shopping. By placing a gun between the girl and her goal, the thief is forcing her to act against her judgment—against her means of survival. If she hands her purse to him, and if he flees without shooting her, she can resume acting on her judgment—but, importantly: *not with respect to the stolen money.* While the thief may be gone, the effect of his force remains. By *keeping* the girl's money, he continues to prevent her from spending it; and *to that extent,* he continues to stop her from acting on her judgment. This ongoing force does not thwart the girl's life totally, but it does thwart her life partially: If she had her money, she would either spend it or save it; but since the thief has her money, she can do neither. She cannot use her money as she chooses, and her life is, to that degree, retarded.

Physical force comes in degrees, and to whatever degree it is used against a person, it impedes his ability to act on his judgment; it prevents him from employing his means of survival; it stops him from living fully as a human being.

Observe further that physical force comes not only in degrees, but also in kinds: *direct,* as in the above examples; and *indirect,* as in the following case.

Suppose a man reads a newspaper advertisement for a used car and goes to check it out. The owner assures the man that the car's odometer reading is correct; this, however, is not true, and the owner knows it because he turned back the mileage himself. As far as the man can tell, though, the owner is being honest, and everything seems to be in order; so he buys the car and drives it away. But notice that the man is *not* driving the car he bargained for; he is not driving the car he was *willing* to buy. Unbeknownst to him, he is driving a different car—one with higher mileage than the one for which he was willing to pay. By lying to the man about the car's mileage and by selling it to him on the basis of that false information, the crook has defrauded the man. Since the man's willingness to exchange his money for the car was based partly on the crook's lie, the crook has gained and is now keeping the man's money against his will. In so doing, the crook is physically forcing the man to act against his judgment. By fraudulently taking and keeping the man's money, the crook is physically preventing him from spending or saving it as he otherwise would.

Fraud, the act of gaining or keeping someone's property by means of deception, is a form of indirect physical force. It *is* physical force, because, although indirect, it physically impedes the victim's ability to act fully on his judgment. Other types of indirect physical force include: *extortion,* the act of gaining or keeping someone's property by distant threat of force; *copyright and patent infringements,* acts of misusing someone's intellectual property (and thus impinging on his ability to act on it); *slander,* the act of making false statements that damage a person's reputation (and thereby retarding his ability to act on it); *unilateral breach of contract,* the act of refusing to deliver goods or services one has agreed to deliver; and so forth. In all such cases, although the force is indirect, it is still physical: When and to the degree it is used, it physically prevents the victim from acting according to his judgment.

Whether direct or indirect, physical force used against a person stops him from living fully as a human being: To the extent it is used, it prevents him from employing his means of survival—the judgment of his mind. And, of course, lone thugs and crooks are not the only perpetrators of such force: Groups and governments can participate, too.

For example, suppose a woman residing in a country under the theocratic rule of the Islamic Taliban (or some similar "authority") decides that she wants to open a restaurant and begins planning the venture. But along comes a Taliban agent who tells the woman that, according to God's law, women are not allowed to run businesses, and that if she attempts to open a restaurant, she will be beaten bloody and thrown in jail. Now the woman cannot act on her judgment. The Taliban's threat poses real physical obstacles—a beating and the walls of a jail—between her thinking and her doing. Her "alternative" is now either to act against her judgment or to be pummeled and caged. In other words, her alternative is to act against her judgment or to act against her judgment: Either she is going to *refrain* from opening a restaurant, or she is going to be pounded and impounded—and thus *restrained* from opening a restaurant. So long as the Taliban's threat is credible, she cannot act on her plan.

Now, what if the agent goes further and tells the woman that, according to God's law, if she seeks even to get a job, she will be beaten and jailed? Then the woman is even more paralyzed. And what if the agent goes still further and says that if she so much as leaves her house she will suffer the same "Holy" consequences? Then the woman is effectively in the same position as are you on the island tied to the tree: completely incapacitated. So long as the Taliban's threat is credible, so long as it is backed by the power to successfully use physical force to stop the woman from acting on her judgment, she cannot act on her judgment; she cannot act as her life requires; she cannot live as a human being. Granted, while confined to her home—if she does not commit suicide, which is what many women who are this oppressed do—she might continue to breathe; but a "life" under house arrest is not a human life. A human life is a life guided by the judgment of one's own mind.

Here is the principle: To whatever degree physical force (or the credible threat thereof) is used against a person, it stops him from acting on his judgment; the greater the force, the less human a life he can live.

Take another example. Suppose a man in communist China wants to start a newspaper that accurately reports to the world the horrific practices of the Chinese government. He diligently investigates the government's activities and gathers some relevant facts surrounding such atrocities as its torturing of political prisoners, its butchering of students in Tiananmen Square, its forcing of women to have abortions, and its drowning of babies in front of their parents. He then begins writing the first edition of his paper, which he plans to print and distribute at large. But the government hears of his plans and sends an official to knock on his door. The official informs the man that, according to the laws of communist China, if he prints one "unfavorable" word about the government, he will be placed in a *laogai* (a "reeducation" prison). Now the man cannot start his newspaper. So long as the Communists have the power to enforce their laws, the man cannot act on his plan. Regardless of whatever else they might permit him to do, he cannot act fully as he thinks he should act; thus, he cannot live fully as a human being.

This is why countless people risk their lives trying to escape from theocratic and communist regimes. Even when such governments are not torturing and slaughtering people for "God's higher purpose" or "society's greater good," their very existence contradicts the basic social requirement of human life: the need of freedom to act on the judgment of one's mind. By physically forcing people to act against their own judgment, such governments make it impossible for them to live fully as human beings. A citizen's consolation for not being murdered by these regimes is a subhuman existence.

The ability to act on one's judgment is an objective requirement of human life. To the extent this ability is impeded, one's life is proportionally retarded.

Now, let us consider some situations in a freer part of the world: the United States.

Suppose a man in Virginia is diagnosed with a deadly disease for which he is told there is no known cure. And suppose the prognosis is that he has only a few months to live. He frantically begins searching for any possible solution to the problem, and soon discovers on the Internet that there is a doctor in New Jersey who claims to have developed an effective treatment for the disease. The man downloads the doctor's research data, reviews it carefully, and feels a sense of relief: In his judgment, the treatment looks quite promising. He calls the doctor and asks to contract with him to begin receiving it immediately. But the doctor informs the man that—as confident as he is about the efficacy of the treatment, and as much as he would like to do business with the man—he cannot dispense the medication, because, if he does, he will go to jail.

"Surely this is some kind of sick humor," says the dying man.

"I wish it were," explains the doctor, "but it is not. The problem is that the so-called experts at the Food and Drug Administration have not approved the treatment; therefore, I am not allowed to prescribe it, and you are not allowed to receive it."

"*What?* Are you telling me that even though I, a dying man, want the treatment and am willing to pay for it—and even though you, a medical doctor, want to treat me and are confident you can save my life—we cannot do business together because some goddamned government agency has not given us *permission?*"

"Regrettably," says the doctor, "that is the case. And shy of changing or breaking the law, there is nothing we can do about it. I'm sorry. Very sorry."

So long as the FDA's regulation exists and is backed by the government's power to enforce it, the medical doctor cannot sell the treatment, and the dying man cannot buy it. Neither man can act as he thinks he should act; neither man can act on the judgment of his own mind; neither man can live fully as a human being; and, consequently, one of them is soon going to die.

The issue of people being forced to act against their own judgment is a matter of life and death. In some cases, such force results in a subhuman existence; in other cases, it means going out of existence; in any event, it is an issue that we who wish to live as human beings need to take seriously. Very seriously.

One more example.

Suppose a company in Seattle develops a software program so useful to people that it renders its rivals' software products obsolete. And suppose the company offers this software for sale on terms that its customers appreciate—but that its rivals do not. Importantly: *The company does not use any kind of physical force against anyone.* Nor does it ask the government to do so. Its customers remain free to negotiate the terms of sale and to buy its products—or not. And its rivals remain free to develop new products and to adjust their terms of sale—or not. In other words, the company deals with its customers only *voluntarily*—by mutual consent and to mutual advantage. And it outperforms its competition solely on *economic* grounds—by creating better software and offering it for sale on shrewder terms.

Unhappy with this situation, the company's rivals pressure the U.S. government to "do something" about what they call the company's "anti-competitive practices," "unfair sales terms," and "predatory pricing." So the government, backed by its massive power to enforce its laws, tells the successful company that according to the latest interpretation of U.S. antitrust law, the company can no longer create and market its software according to its own judgment. "From now on," says the government, "your production procedures and sales terms will be dictated partly by us, the U.S. government. We are going to level the playing field, increase competition, and make terms more fair for everyone."

"But," says the company's CEO, "we have not used any kind of physical force against anyone. We have simply created a product that people like and are selling it to them on terms they are willing to accept. Our competitors are free to compete with us— or not. And our customers are free to buy our products—or not. We do not use clubs or guns; we use logic and trade. What could be more 'level' a playing field than one on which no one uses physical force against anyone? What could be more 'competitive' a market than one in which everyone is free to think and produce to the best of his ability? And what terms could be more 'fair' for everyone than those on which people and businesses *voluntarily* agree to trade?"

"Well," says the government, "it's only natural that you would take such a biased position. After all, you're driven by profit; you're out for your own self-interest. Our antitrust intervention, on the other hand, is altruistic; it's in the best interest of the community; it's for the common good."

"Of course we're driven by profit," says the CEO. "We're a business. And of course we're out for our self-interest. That's what being moral is all about. That's what human life requires. We are not social workers, but software producers. We are not in business for the so-called 'common good'; we are in business for ourselves; we are in business to succeed and grow rich. Anyway, the good of others cannot be achieved by our sacrifice. As Ayn Rand put the principle: 'No one's welfare can be achieved by anyone's sacrifice.' The bottom line is that our products are *our* property—not yours or the 'community's.' So please: Stay out of our way. *Laissez-nous faire.* (Let us alone.)"

"No," says the government. "We are the law around here. Whatever we say goes, and if you don't like it: tough. If we say that you cannot continue to produce and market your software on your own selfish terms, then you can't. If we say that you are going to sacrifice for the whole of which you are merely a part, then that is what you are going to do. That's the law. And if you break it, we'll throw you and your executives in jail."

"But," persists the (unfortunately fictional) CEO, "how can a law be valid when it contradicts the basic social requirement of human life—one's need of freedom to act on one's judgment? How can we *not* be allowed to act as human life requires and *still* be expected to live as human beings? And how can an *American* law be valid when it contradicts the fundamental principle of *America*—the right to life, liberty, and the pursuit of happiness? How can we simultaneously *have* that right and *not* have it? Don't you see the glaring contradictions here?"

"Never mind 'basic requirements,' 'principles,' and 'contradictions,'" says the government. "Your fancy talk will get you nowhere with us. The debate is over. You have been warned."

Clearly, the company can no longer act according to its plans. The threat of physical force—incarceration—has come between its executives' thinking and their doing. They are no longer able to act fully according to their own judgment; they are no longer able to act fully as their life requires; they are no longer able to live fully as human beings.

To the extent physical force is used against people, their ability to function as human beings is impeded if not eliminated. If the force is total—such as in the case of a person being tied to a tree, or held at gunpoint, or placed under house arrest, or carted off to a concentration camp—then it precludes the possibility of human life altogether. And if the force is partial—such as in the case of a person being defrauded, or a doctor and patient being legally forbidden to contract with each other, or a software company being legally forbidden to produce and market its goods according to its own judgment—then it retards human life to that degree. In any case, when physical force is used against a person, he is unable to act fully according to the judgment of his mind; thus, he is unable to live fully as a human being.

Now observe the moral premises underlying the various instances of physical force we have considered. The brute on the island, the mugger with the gun, and the dishonest used-car salesman are acting on the premise of: "I am the moral law. If I say something, it goes." That's personal subjectivism. The Islamic Taliban are acting on the premise of: "God's will is the moral law. If we (God's representatives) say something, it goes." That's "supernatural" subjectivism. The communist Chinese are acting on the premise of: "The Community's will is the moral law. If we (the Community's representatives) say something, it goes." That's social subjectivism. The FDA is acting on the premise of: "Our Agency's will is the medical law. If we (who are expressly not you or your doctor) say that something or other is good or bad for your health, then it is." That's, well, let's just call it a bureaucratic instance of Voltaire's dictum that if we believe in absurdities, we shall commit atrocities.

And on what moral premise is the U.S. government acting in the situation regarding the successful software company? What moral "justification" does the government offer for prohibiting the company's executives from acting on their own judgment?

To review: The government has claimed that it is going to "level the playing field, increase competition, and make terms more fair for everyone." But recall that it has failed to answer the CEO's very straightforward questions: "What could be more 'level' a playing field than one on which no one uses physical force against anyone? What could be more 'competitive' a market than one in which everyone is free to think and produce to the best of his ability? And what terms could be more 'fair' for everyone than those on which people and businesses *voluntarily* agree to trade?" Instead of answering these questions, the government has resorted to the empty claim that its interference in the company's business activities is "for the common good." How does this claim square with the moral principle that no one's welfare can be achieved by anyone's sacrifice? The government has given no answer. Nor has it explained how its use of physical force against the company reconciles with the basic social requirement of human life—or with the fundamental principle of America. In place of all these missing explanations, the government has said blithely: "The debate is over. You have been warned."

So, regardless of the fact that the company has not used any kind of physical force against anyone—regardless of the fact that it has not used any clubs or guns, but only logic and trade—regardless of the fact that it has dealt with its customers only on voluntary terms and has outperformed its rivals solely on economic grounds—the government is nevertheless physically forcing the company to act against its judgment; and the only "justification" the government has given for this use of force is the same one every (secular) despot and dictator in history has given for *their* human sacrifices: "It's in the best interest of the *community.*"

Well, we know the name of that moral premise. And we know its consequences, too.

We have seen that subjectivism in any form—whether personal, "supernatural," or social—leads to human sacrifice. And now we know why: because it leads to people being forced to act against their means of survival—against the judgment of their mind.

In order to live together as civilized beings, rather than suffer and die as sacrificial animals, we must be free to act on our judgment; the only thing that can stop us from doing so is other people; and the only way they can stop us is by means of physical force. Thus, in a social context—in the presence of other people—we need a moral principle to protect us from those who use or attempt to use such force against us. That principle involves the concept of rights.

"Rights," explains Ayn Rand,

> are a *moral* concept—the concept that provides a logical transition from the principles guiding an individual's actions to the principles guiding his relationship with others—the concept that preserves and protects individual morality in a social context—the link between the moral code of a man and the legal code of

a society, between ethics and politics. *Individual rights are the means of subordinating society to moral law.*[1]

A *right* "is a moral principle defining and sanctioning a man's freedom of action in a social context."[2] The key word here is: action. Just as on the personal level we need principles of action to guide us in pursuing our life-serving values, so on the social level we need principles of *interaction* to protect us from those who attempt to interfere with our plans. And just as our ultimate value is our own life, so our fundamental right is our right to our own life. As Ayn Rand put it:

> There is only *one* fundamental right (all others are its consequences or corollaries): a man's right to his own life. Life is a process of self-sustaining and self-generated action; the right to life means the right to engage in self-sustaining and self-generated action—which means: the freedom to take all the actions required by the nature of a rational being for the support, the furtherance, the fulfillment and the enjoyment of his own life. (Such is the meaning of the right to life, liberty and the pursuit of happiness.)[3]

Since human life requires action in accordance with one's own judgment, a person's right to life means his right to take such action—providing he does not violate the same rights of others. Since human life is the standard of moral value, and since human beings are individuals, each person *morally* must be left free to act on his own judgment—and each person *morally* must leave others free to act on theirs.

Whether a person chooses to go fishing, or to build a house, or to go grocery shopping, or to open a restaurant, or to report the news, or to contract with his doctor, or to produce software—he morally must be left free to do so. Each individual has a moral right to his own life, which means: a moral right to act as his life

---

1. Ayn Rand, "Man's Rights," in *The Virtue of Selfishness,* p. 108.
2. Ibid., p. 110.
3. Ibid.

requires, which means: on the judgment of his own mind. And this truth is not limited to our examples. It is a *principle*. It applies to *all* such situations: matters of personal finance, campaign contributions, scientific research, consensual adult sex, abortion, and so on. Each actual (as opposed to potential) individual *owns* himself—body and mind—and has a moral right to act accordingly. (A fetus is a potential individual, not an actual one.)

But, one might ask, what if a person makes stupid, self-destructive decisions?

The right to life is a matter of *self-ownership;* thus, it includes one's freedom to make bad judgments regarding one's own life. Of course, if a person does make bad judgments, he will suffer adverse consequences—which is the reason, in negative terms, why it is crucial to observe reality, consider the relevant facts, be honest, and use logic. But whether an individual's judgment is good or bad, logical or illogical, he still has a moral right to act on it. Since *he* owns himself, he has a moral right to act as *he* chooses—whether rationally or irrationally, honestly or dishonestly, selfishly or selflessly, correctly or incorrectly, competently or incompetently, for better or for worse—*so long as he does not violate the same rights of others.*

For instance, if a person wants to take heroin, he has a moral right to take it; but he has no moral right to steal money from others in order to buy it—and no moral right to harm others while he's on it. Similarly, if a person wants to be dishonest, he has a moral right to do so; hell, if he "feels" like it, he can sit around all day and pretend he's a retired rock star; but he has no moral right to sell someone else's songs under the pretense that *he* wrote them—and no moral right to receive a monthly check from the government to subsidize his fantasy. Likewise, if a person wants to pray, he has a moral right to do so; heck, if he "just believes" he ought to, he can even get on his knees and do it all day; but he has no moral right to force others to pray (not even for a "moment")—and no moral right to allow his child to die of an illness while he (the parent) grovels on the ground instead of seeking medical attention. (Such "parents" should be prosecuted for murder.)

Applying the principle to the corporate arena: If a company wants to hire workers on the basis of some irrelevant characteristic (such as race or sex), rather than on the basis of what is actually important (skill and ability), it has a moral right to do so; but it has no moral right to slander its competitors when they outperform it (as they will) by hiring the more qualified workers it irrationally turns away. Similarly, if a company does not want to compete with rivals of greater ability, it has a moral right *not* to compete with them; but it has no moral right to have government agents cripple its betters. (Such "businessmen" and their accomplices are the moral equivalents of Tonya Harding and hers.)

Now, to be clear, the foregoing is *not* to say that it is in any way moral for a person to take heroin, or kid himself, or speak to "God," or engage in racism, or cower in the face of competition. Moral choices are not synonymous with moral rights. Moral choices pertain to self-interest and rational action in any context in which there are alternatives. Moral rights pertain to self-ownership and freedom of action specifically in a social context. Universally speaking, a person has to act rationally if he wants to live happily; the objective validation of this principle was covered in Chapters 4 through 6. Socially speaking, a person has a moral right to act on his own judgment (be it rational or not), but he has no moral right to physically force others to act against theirs (be *it* rational or not); the objective validation of this principle, in essence, is that when a person is physically forced to act against his judgment, he cannot live fully as a human being.

The right to life *is* one's right to act on one's own judgment—whether good or bad, right or wrong—so long as one does not violate the same rights of others. Correspondingly: The right to *liberty* is one's right to be free from physical interference by other people. The right to *the pursuit of happiness* is one's right to seek the goals and values one chooses. And the right to *freedom of speech* is one's right to express one's thoughts and ideas. These rights are essential to human life; without them we could not live as human beings: Tyranny would reign—as it did in Nazi Germany, Soviet Russia, and theocratic Afghanistan—and as it *does* in theocratic Iran and Sudan as well as in communist China and Cuba. But the above rights depend on yet another right—one without which they, and all other rights, would be meaningless: the right to *property.*

We know that in order to live we have to produce and that in order to produce we have to think. A corollary of these facts is that in order to live we have to be able to keep, use, and dispose of the *things* we produce. Hence the right to property. "The right to life is the source of all rights," explains Ayn Rand, "and the right to property is their only implementation. Without property rights, no other rights are possible. Since man has to sustain his life by his own effort, the man who has no right to the product of his own effort has no means to sustain his life."[4]

To make this point clear, let us return to the island. Suppose the brute unties you from the tree and says: "You may now do as you please—but anything you create is mine—and if you keep, use, or dispose of anything of mine, I'll tie you to the tree again and leave you there to rot." Are you now free to act as your life requires? Not if the brute's threat is credible. Not if he can physically overpower you. If you grow a garden, you cannot eat the vegetables; the brute has already said that the vegetables are *his* and are not to be eaten—or else. If you skin an animal and make a jacket, you cannot wear it; the brute has already said that the jacket is *his* and is not to be worn—or else. If you build a shelter, you cannot enter it; the brute has already said that the shelter is *his* and is not to be entered—or else. No matter what you create, the same physical impediment stands in your way: If you keep, use, or dispose of the product of your effort, you get bound to a tree and left to rot. Thus, you cannot act on the judgment of your mind; you cannot act as your life requires.

As to the issue of degree, suppose the brute says: "Okay, you can keep a third of what you produce, but the other two thirds must be given to me—or else." Then your alternative is to be a corpse or a serf. Granted, as a serf your heart might continue beating for a while; but a "life" of serfdom is not a human life. A human life is a life guided by the judgment of one's own mind.

Without the right to the product of one's effort, one cannot live as a human being. Thus, in a social context, individual rights—*including property rights*—are an objective requirement of human life.

---

4. Ibid.

Now, legally speaking, what does all of this come down to? What basic legal principles can we draw from this abundance of evidence?

Clearly, if people are to live as civilized beings, rather than as barbarians, they must respect and not violate one another's rights. Likewise, if a government is to defend liberty, rather than advance tyranny, it must protect and not violate its citizen's rights. So the question is: What principles, if upheld, could ensure that individual rights would be respected, protected, and not violated?

Well, as Ayn Rand observed, and as we can now see: "Man's rights can be violated only by the use of physical force. It is only by means of physical force that one man can deprive another of his life, or enslave him, or rob him, or prevent him from pursuing his own goals, or compel him to act against his own rational judgment." Accordingly:

> The precondition of a civilized society is the barring of physical force from social relationships—thus establishing the principle that if men wish to deal with one another, they may do so only by means of *reason*: by discussion, persuasion and voluntary, uncoerced agreement.[5]

Thus, the basic legal principle of a civilized society is that "no man may *initiate* the use of physical force against others." The operative word here being: initiate.

> No man—or group or society or government—has the right to assume the role of a criminal and initiate the use of physical compulsion against any man. Men have the right to use physical force *only* in retaliation and *only* against those who initiate its use. The ethical principle involved is simple and clear-cut: it is the difference between murder and self defense. A holdup man seeks to gain a value, wealth, by killing his victim; the victim does not grow richer by killing a holdup man. The principle is: no man may obtain any values from others by resorting to physical force.[6]

---

5. Ayn Rand, "The Nature of Government," in *The Virtue of Selfishness*, p. 126.
6. Rand, "The Objectivist Ethics," p. 36.

A civilized society is one in which people are legally free to act on their own judgment, which means: free to produce whatever they choose to produce, however they choose to produce it; free to contract with others and engage in ventures of any kind and scale; free to form companies and corporations of any size and structure; free to offer their goods and services to others on whatever terms they deem appropriate; free to deal with people and businesses on whatever terms they mutually and voluntarily agree to trade; free to achieve as much as they are willing and able to achieve; and free to keep, use, and dispose of the products of their own efforts. The only thing that people are *not* legally "free" to do in such a society is to initiate physical force against other people.

Now, an important implication of this principle is that there can be no such thing as a right to be *given* goods or services, because such a "right" on the part of one person necessarily entails a violation of rights on the part of another. If a person has a "right" to be given food, someone has to be *forced* to prepare it for him. If he has a "right" to be given money, someone has to be *forced* to earn it for him. If he has a "right" to be given a job, someone has to be *forced* to hire him. If he has a "right" to be given a home, someone has to be *forced* to build it for him. If he has a "right" to be given an education, someone has to be *forced* to teach him. If he has a "right" to be given health care, someone has to be *forced* to provide it for him. And so on.

Of course, parents have a *chosen* and thus *moral* responsibility to care properly for their children. But that is another matter.

The point here is simply that human values are not free; they do not come ready-made in nature; they are not just out there for the taking; they must be *produced*. And, as Ayn Rand put it: "The man who produces while others dispose of his product is a slave."[7]

If some men are entitled by right to the products of the work of others, it means that those others are deprived of rights and condemned to slave labor. Any alleged "right" of one man which necessitates the violation of the rights of another, is not and

---

7. Rand, "Man's Rights," p. 110.

cannot be a right. No man can have a right to impose an unchosen obligation, an unwarranted duty or an involuntary servitude on another man. There can be no such thing as *"the right to enslave."*[8]

A right that violates a right is a contradiction in terms. Just as green is not red, just as stop does not mean go, and just as a bush cannot speak, so a right cannot violate a right. Each individual is morally an end in himself—not a means to the ends of others. Accordingly, in order to live as a moral being (rather than as a parasite), each individual must *produce* the values on which his life depends. He may trade his products with others, but he may not steal products from others. He may offer his goods and services for exchange or as gifts, but he may not compel others to buy or accept them. He may ask others for assistance, but he may not make them help him. And he may compete in a free market, but he may not attack his rivals—or have the government do so.

The reason is clear: The use (or threat) of physical force against human beings impedes the basic requirement of their life—their ability to act on their own judgment. Thus, the initiation of physical force against people—in any form or degree—is factually immoral and properly illegal.

A *moral* society is one in which the use of initiatory physical force against human beings is prohibited by law. And the only social system in which such force *is* so prohibited is pure, *laissez-faire* capitalism. (*Laissez faire* is French for *let do,* as in: Let people do as they choose.)

"Laissez-faire capitalism," explains Ayn Rand, "is a system where men deal with one another, not as victims and executioners, nor as masters and slaves, but as *traders,* by free, voluntary exchange to mutual benefit. It is a system where no man may obtain any values from others by resorting to physical force, and *no man may initiate the use of physical force against others."*[9]

A related and essential feature of laissez-faire capitalism is its unique position on property. Pure capitalism "is a social system

---

8. Ibid., p. 113.
9. Rand, "Introducing Objectivism," p. 4.

based on the recognition of individual rights, including property rights, in which all property is privately owned."[10] In a laissez-faire society, people are fully free to act on their own judgment and thus to produce, keep, use, and dispose of their own property as they see fit. What makes such freedom possible is that all property is private. Since there is no "public" property, there is no need for the government to forcibly take money from citizens in order to acquire or maintain such property. And since all property is private, disputes over what people can do and where they can do it are quickly resolved by simply asking: Whose property is in question? Under pure capitalism, individual rights, including property rights, are protected by the government and cannot be legally violated by anyone—including the government.

That is not and cannot be the case in a society where "public" property exists. Since "public" property is paid for with money taken by the government from citizens under threat of force—and since such property is owned by "everyone in general" and thus by no one in particular—its very existence *constitutes* a violation of individual rights. In addition to the fact that the government steals money from citizens in order to acquire and maintain such property, since no one in particular owns it, no one has a right to say what anyone can do with or on it—even though it supposedly belongs to everyone. Not surprisingly, this results in a torrent of conflicting rights-claims and irresolvable rights-disputes.

Observe, for example, the heated and endless debates in the United States over issues ranging from whether or not people should have to wear seatbelts on "public" roads—to what kind of art should be shown in "public" galleries or paid for with "public" funds—to what should be taught in and whether or not children should have to pray in "public" schools—to what should be done with natural resources such as trees and oil on "public" land. In all such cases, the problem is that the property in question is "public." Such property creates a never-ending battle in which no one's rights are fully protected and everyone's rights are partially violated.

---

10. Ayn Rand, "What is Capitalism?" in *Capitalism: The Unknown Ideal* (New York: Signet, 1967), p. 19.

In a laissez-faire society, however—a society in which all property is privately owned—individual rights are recognized as *inalienable,* which means: *absolute.* People can do anything they please with and on their own property; they are forbidden only to infringe on the rights of others. In addition to eliminating the government's need to steal money from citizens to pay for "public" property, this principle makes perfectly clear who has a right to decide what will be done with or on any given piece of property. If a person (or company or corporation) owns a road, *he* says whether or not people have to wear seatbelts on it; others can accept his rules, or drive on another road, or fly in an airplane, or take a train. If a person owns an art gallery, *he* decides what kind of art will be shown there; others can patronize his gallery or not. If a person wants to support a certain kind of art, he can put *his* money where *his* values are, but he cannot force others to put *their* money there. If a person owns a school, *he* decides what will be taught there and whether or not the students will be required to pray. People who do not like his curriculum or policies can suggest that he change them, or send their children to a different school, or start their own school, or teach their children at home. If a person owns land, *he* determines how it and its contents will be used. He can build roads, homes, schools, hospitals, shopping centers, business parks, or entire communities on it; or he can harvest trees, create a lake, produce electricity, develop a theme park, grow crops, engage in research, dig a landfill, build a water-treatment plant, raise chickens, drill for oil, or "leave it alone." And whatever he decides to do—so long as he does not violate the rights of others—no one can force him to do otherwise, because in a truly capitalist society, no one, including the government, is allowed to violate anyone's rights.

"The only function of the government, in such a society," continues Ayn Rand, "is the task of protecting man's rights, *i.e.,* the task of protecting him from physical force; the government acts as the agent of man's right of self-defense, and may use force only in retaliation and only against those who initiate its use."[11]

---

11. Ibid.

The citizens of a laissez-faire society delegate the use of re-taliatory force to the government and thus make domestic peace possible. Of course, in an emergency situation, or when the police are not available, or when there is no time to rely on the govern-ment, citizens are morally and legally justified in using retaliatory force as necessary to protect themselves, their property, or other people from aggressors. But in order to live together as civilized beings (rather than as feuding hillbillies), people must leave such force to the government whenever possible: "The government is the means of placing the retaliatory use of force under *objective control*."[12]

In a capitalist society, if someone physically harms a person or damages his property or threatens to do either—and if this can be demonstrated by means of evidence—then the victim has grounds for legal recourse and, when appropriate, compensation. If someone defrauds a man, or threatens to murder him, or dumps trash in his yard, or cuts down his trees, or blows up his labora-tory, or poisons his water supply, or infringes on his patent, or spews noxious fumes into his lungs, or steals his bag of crystals, or vandalizes his oil rig—or in any other way causes him or his property specific harm—then the perpetrator has violated the man's rights. And if the man (or an agent on his behalf) can demonstrate that the perpetrator has done so—by presenting evidence to that effect—then he has a case against the rights violator and can seek justice in a court of law.

If, however, a person alleges that his (or someone else's) rights have been violated but presents *no* evidence in support of his claim, then he has *no* case. A claim backed by no evidence is an arbitrary, *subjective* claim. The basic principle of *objective* law in this regard is that people must present evidence in support of their accusations. It obviously cannot be otherwise. Imagine a society in which anyone's mere assertion that a person or group commit-ted a crime would warrant the arrest and indictment of the ac-cused by a government that regards evidence as unnecessary in le-gal proceedings.

---

12. Ibid.

Citizen: "I say that toxins emitted into the air by Nader, Hillary & Gore, Incorporated caused me to develop cancer—and I want justice."

Government: "Okay, we will arrest and try the company's executives for violating your rights." (I'll let the reader take it from here, but remember: The claimant presents no evidence, and the courts do not require any—just like the Salem witch trials.)

In a laissez-faire society, people are free to do what they choose with their own lives and property; they are forbidden to physically harm others or *their* property; and they are required to support their allegations with evidence. Laissez-faire capitalism is the system of individual rights, private property, and *objective law.* Objective laws are laws that are grounded in the factual requirements of human life and that uphold the principles of logic; thus, they protect individual rights, including property rights, and they recognize that the burden of proof is on he who asserts that rights have been violated.

Accordingly, if a person (or company or corporation) *does* violate an individual's rights—and if this is shown to be the case in a court of law—then the government takes action against the perpetrator as necessary on two counts: first, to provide his victim with recompense when and as appropriate; second, to punish the rights-violator for and in proportion to any crime he has committed.

So, what does all of this say about the moral status of capitalism?

Well, on one level it says that capitalism is the system of justice—which is to say a lot. But on a deeper level, it says even more. Since capitalism is the only social system in which the courts uphold the principles of objective law—since it is the only social system in which the government protects individual rights (including property rights)—since it is the only social system in which people can act fully according to their own judgment and thus live fully as human beings—*capitalism is the only moral social system.*

But, one might ask, what about the poor, the disabled, and the helpless? How do they fare under laissez-faire?

To answer this question, we must bear in mind that very few people are genuinely helpless or unable to support themselves; the great majority of people *are* capable of acting as their life requires. And if a person chooses to live and *is* capable of supporting himself, he has a moral responsibility to do so; if he refuses to support himself and, instead, steals, begs, or seeks handouts, he is acting parasitically and immorally.

With this in mind, let us consider the position of the poor, the disabled, and the helpless in a truly capitalist system. But we must take them one at a time, for they are not necessarily one and the same.

As to the poor: Capitalism leaves each individual free to think, work, and make as much money as he is willing and able to earn. No other social system on earth does this. In a capitalist society, if a poor person wants to work his way out of poverty—as countless poor people have done—he is *fully* free to do so. Of course, if he doesn't want to, he doesn't have to; the choice is his to make, and no one can force him one way or the other.

Some people are not concerned with being wealthy, but this does not make them immoral. While an artist or a gardener might be financially poor, he is not by that fact less moral than a CEO or an athlete who is financially rich. A person's monetary wealth does not determine his moral status. His choices and actions do: Are they rational or irrational—life-promoting or life-retarding, selfish or selfless, honest or dishonest? Morally speaking, *that* is what matters. If having more money is honestly important to a person, he should act accordingly by, for instance, seeking a higher-paying job, investing his money more wisely, or starting a business of his own. And capitalism not only leaves everyone—including the poor—completely free to do so; it also provides an ever-increasing flow of educational possibilities and moneymaking opportunities.

As to the disabled: Capitalism leaves them free to compensate for their disabilities by means of any remaining abilities they might have. Again, no other social system on earth does this. In a capitalist society, if a person lacks ability in some respect but still has abilities in other respects, he is *fully* free to use his existing abilities to support and further his life—as many disabled people do. For instance: A deaf person might choose to pursue a career in genetics, architecture, or accounting. A blind person might choose to pursue a career in music, radio, or psychology. A paraplegic might choose to pursue a career in law, education, or writing. And today—with the technology made possible by freer markets—even a quadriplegic can learn to support himself; he might pursue a career in finance, economics, or computer programming.

When disabled people are fully free to act on their judgment, there is usually something they can do to compensate for their shortcomings. And capitalism not only leaves them completely free to do so; it also makes available an ever-increasing flow of enabling technology.

Now, as to the helpless: It is crucial here to acknowledge that very few people actually fall into this extremely unfortunate category. At this point, we are talking only about people who are *severely* retarded, have a *totally* debilitating disease, or are injured to the extent that they are unable to support themselves by *any* means. What happens to such people in a laissez-faire society? Capitalism leaves each individual free to offer them as much charity as he is able and willing to offer. Once again, no other social system on earth does this. In a capitalist society, if a person has the means and the desire to assist the helpless—as many people do—he is *fully* free to do so. Of course, if he *doesn't* have the means, he *can't* offer them assistance. And whether he has the means or not, if he doesn't want to, he doesn't have to; the choice is his to make, and no one can force him one way or the other.

But, one might wonder, what if everyone's rights are respected, yet no one wants to help the helpless.

As always, to address this concern we must observe the relevant facts. What the helpless need but cannot produce is life-serving values; that's what makes them helpless. Such values can be produced only by able people; hence the term able. But able people can produce values only if they are *free* to act on the very thing that makes them able: their judgment. The basic social condition that makes human life possible is *freedom*—freedom from the initiation of physical force—the freedom of each individual to act on the judgment of his own mind.

Thus, respect for individual rights is as much in the best interest of the helpless as it is in the best interest of the able—if not more so. Think about it: If the able are not free, they cannot live (as human beings); and if the able cannot live, what happens to the helpless? Clearly, if the helpless are to be helped, they (and everyone who cares about them) must respect individual rights—including the rights of the able.

Observe further that while in reality there are very few genuinely helpless people, when individual rights are respected there are plenty of people who are willing and able to help them. Look around: Do you ever see people working with the mentally retarded? Ask your friends: Would they ever donate money to help a poor child with leukemia? Ask yourself: Would you ever offer assistance to a victim of a devastating accident? Consider this: Even in the semi-free, mixed economy of the United States today—in which producers are heavily and immorally taxed—the amount of money voluntarily donated to charity is enormous; in 1999 alone, tax-strapped Americans gave over *$190 billion* to charity.[13]

But, one might suppose, isn't that because people are partly altruistic and not fully selfish? Why would a *true* egoist ever want to help the helpless?

To be sure, a truly selfish person would not offer "help" to bums who in fact are *not* "helpless" but rather *choose* to be parasites. Only a fool or an altruist would do that. But to answer the question of why an egoist would ever want to help people who genuinely cannot support themselves, we need only consider the alternatives—of which there are two: A person can either help the helpless or not help them. So here is the question every egoist has to answer for himself. Which environment do I think is in my best interest: one in which genuinely helpless people suffer and die in the streets, or one in which I voluntarily contribute some small fraction of my time, effort, or money to give them a hand?

I certainly know which environment is in *my* best interest, and I imagine you know which is in yours. But this is something every individual has to decide for himself—and no one has a moral right to force him one way or the other. Fortunately, the decision does not require advanced mathematics; it merely requires genuine self-interest, reverence for human life, and basic logic.

---

13. See the American Association of Fundraising Counsel (www.aafrc.org).

Rational egoism, true egoism, does *not* say: "Be indifferent to other human beings" or "Don't help people." It says: "If one wants to live as a human being and achieve genuine happiness, one must observe reality; one must think; one must not accept contradictions; one must pursue one's life-serving values; one must not surrender greater values for the sake of lesser ones; one must be honest; one must have integrity"; and so on. If a person thinks that helping certain other people is in his best interest, he should act accordingly. And capitalism not only leaves everyone completely free to do so; it also enables people to create enormous amounts of surplus wealth with which to do it.

When people are free to produce as much wealth as they are able and willing to produce—and free to do with their wealth whatever they choose to do with it—many people become very rich. Add to this the fact that truly self-interested people care about human life—they, after all, are the ones who recognize that it is the standard of moral value—and thus do not want other human beings to suffer and die needlessly, and we have a clear answer to the question, "What if no one wants to help the helpless?" The concern is simply unwarranted. The fact is that many people—including presumably the people who ask the question—*do* want to help the helpless. And in a truly capitalist society, no one would be allowed to stop them.

Now, let us conclude this chapter by acknowledging some of the broad social and legal implications of the moral truths we have discovered.

We have seen that, in a social context, individual rights, including property rights, are essential to human life. Without them, we cannot act fully on our own judgment; we cannot live fully as human beings. A proper government is one that recognizes this fact and proceeds accordingly. "The only proper, *moral* purpose of a government," writes Ayn Rand, "is to protect man's rights, which means: to protect him from physical violence—to protect his right to his own life, to his own liberty, to his own *property* and to

---

14. Rand, "The Objectivist Ethics," p. 36.

the pursuit of his own happiness."[14] And: "Since the protection of individual rights is the only proper purpose of a government, it is the only proper subject of legislation: all laws must be based on individual rights and aimed at their protection."[15] Proper laws, moral laws, *objective* laws are laws that are thus based and so aimed.

Laws that protect individual rights—such as those against murder, rape, child abuse, patent infringements, fraud, and slander—are objective laws; they morally must be upheld by citizens and enforced by the government. Laws that violate individual rights—such as those that mandate "community" or "national" service, those that abridge the freedom of production and trade, those that restrict doctors and patients from contracting with one another, those that forcibly redistribute wealth, those that prohibit acts of consensual adult sex, those that presume a fetus (a potential individual) has any prerogatives over a woman (an actual individual), and those that block any kind of scientific research—are subjective laws; they morally must be condemned by citizens and repealed by the government. None of this is a matter of personal opinion or social convention or divine revelation; it is all a matter of observable fact—the observable fact that freedom from the initiation of physical force is an objective requirement of human life.

Whereas rational egoism guides our choices and actions in pursuit of our life-serving goals and long-term happiness, laissez-faire capitalism protects individual rights by banning the initiation of physical force from social relationships. The two go hand in hand. The first makes human *existence* possible; the second makes human *coexistence* possible. As Ayn Rand put it: "What greater virtue can one ascribe to a social system than the fact that it leaves no possibility for any man to serve his own interests by enslaving other men? What nobler system could be desired by anyone whose goal is man's well-being?"[16]

---

15. Rand, "The Nature of Government," p. 128.
16. Ayn Rand, "Theory and Practice," in *Capitalism: The Unknown Ideal*, p. 136.

8

Concluding Summary
What We Now Know

The purpose of this book has been twofold: 1) to show that morality is a matter not of divine revelation or social convention or personal opinion—but, rather, of the factual requirements of human life and happiness; and 2) to show what, in essence, those requirements are.

We have seen that the claim "If there is no God, anything goes" is false. Morally speaking, *nothing goes*—except actions that promote human life. And since human beings are individuals—each with his own body, his own mind, his own life—moral actions are *selfish* actions—actions taken by an individual to promote his *own* life.

The false alternative of religion versus subjectivism has been exposed: Religion is a form of subjectivism. But this is not a problem, because just as there is no evidence for the existence of God, so there is no *need* for him. We don't need him for a standard of morality, because human life is logically the standard of morality. We don't need him for purpose or meaning, because we choose our own purposes; thus, the meaning of our life is whatever we make of it. In short, we don't need God for guidance, because—if we choose to use it—our rational judgment tells us what is true or false, good or bad, right or wrong.

The is–ought problem has been solved: Since life is the standard of value, if we choose to live, then reality (what *is*) dictates what we *ought* to do—we ought to take the actions necessary to sustain and further our life.

Morality is not subjective, but *objective;* it is not created by the human mind, but *discovered* by it. Just as truth is discovered by reference to evidence and the principle of non-contradiction, so morality is discovered by reference to the requirements of human life and the principle of non-sacrifice. While a person or group might have faith or feel that drinking Drano is "good" or that dishonesty "pays" or that human sacrifice is "the way to go," neither faith nor feelings—individually or collectively—can change the nature of reality or the factual requirements of human life and happiness.

Morality is a matter of observation, logic, and the law of causality. It is black and white, either/or, through and through. It is an immutable fact that to live as human beings we have to observe the laws of nature and think; hence the objective value of *reason.* It is an immutable fact that if we want to sustain and further our life, we have to choose and pursue life-promoting goals; hence the objective value of *purpose.* And it is an immutable fact that if we want to accomplish our goals and achieve genuine happiness, we have to earn and maintain the conviction that we are able to live and worthy of success; hence the objective value of *self-esteem.* These three—reason, purpose, and self-esteem—are the fundamental requirements of human life and happiness; thus, they are the basic moral values.

Correspondingly, virtues are the kinds of actions that sustain and further human life; vices are the kinds of actions that retard or destroy it. Thus, right versus wrong is a matter of rationality vs. irrationality, productiveness vs. parasitism, honesty vs. dishonesty, integrity vs. hypocrisy, independent thinking vs. second-handedness, justice vs. injustice, pride vs. humility. Moral virtues are the basic actions that account for the objective requirements of human life; they are the *principled* actions on which human life depends.

To live as a human being, one must identify and satisfy numerous long-range and wide-range needs—both material and spiritual—and (fundamentally speaking) there is only one way to do it: by thinking rationally and acting accordingly.

While nothing can compel a person to be moral, the unalterable fact is that the only way to live and achieve genuine happiness *is* by being moral—by consistently choosing, planning, and pursuing rational, life-promoting values—by being genuinely self-interested as a matter of principle. What each person chooses to do is up to him, and the consequences of his choices and actions are his: either to suffer or to enjoy.

Rational egoism is the only morality that is *for* human life; thus, it is the only morality that is actually moral. Those who choose to be rationally self-interested thereby make the most of their life—and they are morally good because of it.

In the realm of politics, rational self-interest requires recognition of the fact that in order to *take* life-promoting action, one must be *free* to do so; one must be free to act on the judgment of one's mind. The only thing that can stop one from doing so is other people, and the only way they can do it is by means of physical force.

In order to live together as civilized beings, rather than as barbarians—in order to coexist as independent equals, rather than as masters and slaves—people have to refrain from using physical force against one another. Hence the principle of individual rights: Each person *morally* must be left free to act according to his own judgment—so long as he does not violate the same rights of others.

A moral society—a civilized society—is one that bans the use of *initiatory* physical force from human relationships and delegates the use of *retaliatory* force to the government for the sole purpose of protecting individual rights. Accordingly, such a society prohibits its government from using physical force except in retaliation against those who initiate (or threaten) its use. And the only social system that does so—thereby leaving people free to act *fully* as human life requires—is pure, laissez-faire capitalism.

Just as rational egoism is the only morality that is actually moral, so laissez-faire capitalism is the only social system that is actually moral. And just as the first leads to the second, so the second depends on the first. Egoism and capitalism mutually imply each other; to uphold either consistently, one must uphold both unwaveringly.

It all comes down to this: Do you want to live in a world in which you are free to choose and pursue your own goals and values; free to do with your own body, your own mind, your own life, whatever you think is in your best interest; free to engage with other adults in whatever kinds of relationships you and they agree to engage in; free to think, work, and achieve whatever you are willing and able to achieve; free to keep, use, and dispose of the products of your own efforts; free to trade your goods and services with others voluntarily, by mutual consent and to mutual advantage; free to act according to your own judgment in *all* areas of your life; free to live *fully* as a human being? In short: Do you want to make the most of your life and achieve the greatest happiness possible?

If so, you must embrace, advocate, and defend laissez-faire capitalism; the principle of individual rights; and the ethics on which they, your life, and your happiness depend: rational egoism—the morality of self-interest. It is supported by the facts of reality. It is required for human existence. It is a matter of loving life.

Afterword

Terrorism, Altruism, and Moral Certainty

Loving Life is based on Ayn Rand's philosophy of Objectivism, which she called "a philosophy for living on earth." In the midst of our war against terrorists and the governments that support them, the importance of a philosophy for living on earth could not be more apparent—or more urgent.

> The conflict has reached its ultimate climax; the choice is clear-cut: either a new morality of rational self-interest, with its consequences of freedom, justice, progress and man's happiness on earth—or the primordial morality of altruism, with its consequences of slavery, brute force, stagnant terror and sacrificial furnaces.[1]

Ayn Rand wrote those words in 1960. If only more people had faced the facts of morality back then.

Islamic terrorists are religious altruists: They selflessly commit human sacrifices for the sake of a supernatural "other"—an alleged God. The essential solution to the problem of terrorism (whether religious or secular) is the same antidote needed to

---

1. Ayn Rand, *For the New Intellectual*, p. 54.

counter any form of human sacrifice: a proper morality. As Ayn Rand explained, and as we now know: "The creed of sacrifice is a morality for the immoral."[2] A proper morality—a morality for the *moral*—is a code of non-sacrifice: the morality of *life*.

If we want to protect our lives and our loved ones from murderous aggressors, if we want to defeat terrorists (or any such evil), military superiority is not enough. In a battle against evil, military superiority is a necessary condition, but it is not a sufficient condition; we also, and more fundamentally, need *moral certainty*. If we are to win this war, we need to be morally certain that we have the absolute right to annihilate terrorists and their sponsors by any means necessary. And the only source of (genuine) moral certainty is an observation-based, non-contradictory, rationally provable, *objective* code of values. Fortunately, we now have one. The question is: Will we proudly embrace it, or will we humbly allow the creed of sacrifice to continue mowing us down? Will we act resolutely and finish the job that must be done, or will we act timidly and take only partial measures? Will we defend ourselves properly and destroy *all* known terrorists as well as *all* governments known to support terrorism, or will we act with "restraint," surrender to "world opinion," and allow some of them to remain in existence, to continue plotting attacks against us, and to slaughter more innocent people in the future?

The only way to summon the moral courage to do what obviously needs to be done is to possess the moral certainty that it is objectively the right thing to do. And the only way to possess such certainty is to know what you now know.

I urge you to tell people about the objective morality you have discovered. Give this book to your friends. Read Ayn Rand's books. Give *them* to your friends. Tell everyone you know that "There *is* a morality of reason, a morality proper to man, and *Man's Life* is its standard of value."[3] As Ayn Rand said: "The world is ours, whenever we choose to claim it, by virtue and grace of the fact that ours is the Morality of Life."[4]

---

2. Ibid., p. 141.
3. Ibid., p. 122.
4. Ibid., p. 169.

Appendix

Emergency Situations
The Principle Remains

I have relegated the subject of emergencies to an appendix because—contrary to the approach of some ethics professors who treat the subject as if it were the central issue in morality—it is, in fact, only an afterthought in the field.

Logically, we can apply moral principles to emergency situations only *after* we have discovered and validated such principles. And the discovery and validation of moral principles require a process of rational thinking applied to the requirements of normal, everyday human life—such as those examined in the main body of this book. Now that we *do* have a set of valid moral principles, we can address the subject of emergencies quickly and easily.

An emergency is an unexpected and serious situation that requires immediate action. What makes a situation serious and require immediate action? The fact that it has serious and immediate bearing on *human life*. In other words, like all moral concepts, the concept of "emergency" presupposes and depends on the principle that human life is the standard of moral value. Detached from this base, the concept is meaningless.

Thus, while an emergency is an unusual situation, the basic principle of proper conduct when faced with one remains: If a person wants to live as a human being, he has to act in a rational, self-interested manner. As Ayn Rand put it, the rational principle of conduct is: "Always act in accordance with the hierarchy of your values, and never sacrifice a greater value to a lesser one."[1] Emergencies are no exception to this principle; they are just urgent situations in which, to be moral, a person must be rationally self-interested under extraordinary circumstances.

In all situations, emergencies included, *moral action* is *selfish action*—action that, according to one's own rational, independent judgment, is in one's best interest. As to how this principle applies in any particular situation (whether ordinary or extraordinary), the only person who can decide is each individual involved; the only person he can decide for is himself; and the only way he can decide is by reference to the available and relevant facts—the full context of his knowledge, values, abilities, commitments, and alternatives.

Should I (an able swimmer) jump into the river to save my lover, who just fell in and cannot swim—or should I allow her to drown? What would be the selfish thing to do?

Should I (an armed father) shoot the kidnapper who just stuffed my child into his car and is now running around to the driver's side—or should I watch him get in and drive away? What would be in my best interest?

Should we (the United States of America) annihilate the governments that have sponsored terrorism against Americans—or should we pretend that they aren't evil, didn't mean any harm, and won't do it anymore? What would be in our best interest?

Should I (a bodyguard, policeman, or Marine) protect the people under attack whom I have voluntarily contracted to protect—or should I run away? What would be consistent with my chosen values?

It is all a matter of honesty, integrity, and justice—in a word: rationality.

As to whether it can ever be proper to risk one's life in order to save the life of a stranger whom one is *not* under contract to protect, it still depends on one's own independent judgment with respect to the available and relevant facts. Would the rescue at-

---

1. Rand, "The Ethics of Emergencies," p. 50.

tempt constitute a sacrifice of one's values? If so, it would be immoral; if not, it would be morally permissible. Does one think one is capable of the mission? If so, it would be morally permissible; if not, it would be immoral suicide. Would one be doing it out of selfish *reverence* for human potential—or selfless "duty" to serve others? The first motive is moral; the second is evil.

To be moral, one must be *selfish*—emergencies included.

Now, what if a person is faced with a serious predicament in which, according to his own rational judgment, none of his alternatives appears to be any more or less self-interested than do any of his others? Then he is not in an emergency situation, but at a moral impasse.

A *moral impasse* is a situation in which moral concepts—such as "right" and "wrong," "should" and "shouldn't"—are not applicable because, given the circumstances, they are stripped of all meaning.

The realm of morality is the realm of *choice*—choice regarding that which is *for* or *against* one's life as a rational being. Moral concepts can have meaning to a person only when he can discern a rationally self-interested difference among his alternatives. When no such difference can be seen, no moral choice can be made.

Look at it this way: How can a choice be "selfish" if the person who makes it does not think it is in his best interest to do so? Obviously it can't. Thus, if a person is faced with a situation in which he cannot determine a rationally self-interested course of action, any "choice" he makes regarding the predicament is outside the realm of moral judgment.

Such situations are popular with subjectivist college professors, who present them to unwary students in an effort to convince them that there are no right or wrong answers to moral questions. A typical dilemma goes as follows. (I apologize in advance for bringing this image to your mind, but it is the kind of example offered in some of the so-called ethics textbooks in use today.)

> You are an inmate in a concentration camp. A sadistic guard is about to hang your son who tried to escape and wants you to pull the chair from underneath him. He says that if you don't he

will not only kill your son but some other innocent inmate as
well. You don't have any doubt that he means what he says.
What should you do?[2]

The answer to this (and to *all* such questions in *all* such situations) is: *There is no "should" about it.* This is a moral impasse;
any "choice" one makes regarding it is logically outside the realm
of moral judgment. (A professor's choice to pose such a question
in an effort to propagate moral skepticism, however, is not.)

Lastly, it is worth emphasizing that, while bad things can and
sometimes do happen in life, in a moral society—one that respects
and protects individual rights—disasters are not the rule but the
exception; emergencies are extremely rare, and moral impasses are
even rarer. In a capitalist society, life consists primarily of opportunities to choose among better and worse alternatives; to pursue
and achieve selfish, life-promoting goals; and to do so with the
comforts of technology and in the company of civilized people.
Moral principles are essential to the whole process. While we occasionally need them in order to deal with emergency situations,
we continually need them in order to live and love life.

---

2. Victor Grassian, *Moral Reasoning* (Englewood Cliffs: Prentice Hall, 1992),
   p. 6; similar examples can be found on pp. 6–10 and in other college texts.

Recommended Reading

Ayn Rand, *Atlas Shrugged.* A brilliant suspense novel about the role of the mind in human life, and about what happens to the world when the thinkers and producers mysteriously disappear.

————, *The Fountainhead.* An inspiring, heroic novel about an independent and uncompromising architect.

————, *Philosophy: Who Needs It.* Essays on the life-and-death importance of philosophy.

————, *For the New Intellectual.* A brief outline of Ayn Rand's philosophy, including the main philosophic passages from her novels.

————, *The Virtue of Selfishness.* A revolutionary book on the foundation, essence, and meaning of rational egoism.

————, *Capitalism: The Unknown Ideal.* What we all should have been taught in school about capitalism but were not. A comprehensive moral defense of the only social system consistent with the requirements of human life.

Leonard Peikoff, *Objectivism: The Philosophy of Ayn Rand.* One of the most important books ever written. An accurate, systematic, and comprehensive presentation of Ayn Rand's philosophy.

————, *The Ominous Parallels.* An objective (and alarming) analysis of the ideas that gave rise to Nazi Germany—and the ongoing propagation of these same ideas in American universities.

The Objective Standard, a quarterly journal of culture and politics written from an Objectivist perspective: www.TheObjectiveStandard.com.

Index

About The Author

Craig Biddle is the editor of *The Objective Standard*, a journal of culture and politics written from an Objectivist perspective. He is currently writing a book about the principles of good thinking and the fallacies that are violations of those principles. His lectures and courses on epistemology, ethics, and individual rights are available from the Ayn Rand Bookstore and from his website, www.CraigBiddle.com.